HOMEBODIES

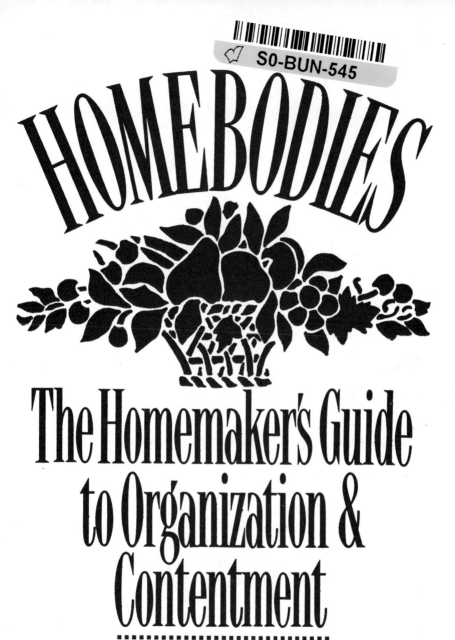

The Homemaker's Guide to Organization & Contentment

Linda Davis Zumbehl

Homebodies

Linda Davis Zumbehl

© 1991
Printed in the United States of America
ISBN: 0-88368-220-6

Editorial assistance for Whitaker House by Debra Petrosky

Cover design by Terry Dugan

Unless otherwise noted, Scripture quotations are taken from the *New American Standard Bible,* copyright © The Lockman Foundation, 1960, 1962, 1963, 1968, 1971, 1972, 1973, 1975, 1977 and used by permission. Scripture quotations marked KJV are from the *King James Version* of the Bible.

Dedication

I gratefully dedicate this book to Betty Davis, my mother, with appreciation for her love, devotion, and for being there whenever I need her . . . and to Florence Zumbehl, my mother-in-law, for being a consistent source of kindness and blessing for all these years. I thank God for both of you!

Contents

Contents

Acknowledgements

Many thanks to all those who assisted in the writing of this book with their encouragement, feedback, and prayers, including Geri Bowen, Paula DeGarmo, Cathy Harding, Barb LeGare, Dee McDonald, Kim Milberg, Fritzi Smith . . . and a special thank you to Debra Petrosky for her editing persistence.

Introduction

"Lord, what on earth is the matter with me?" I muttered. I was having one of those discussions with God that I often have in frustrating moments. As I wove my way through the bustling morning traffic on my way to work, nothing seemed at all right. I was growing more and more dissatisfied with life in the fast track.

"Here I am complaining when You've given me the job I always thought I wanted. I have a management position, my own office, and I work with nice people—and yet I'm not satisfied. Why am I really happy only when I'm home?"

Suddenly God did something that never ceases to surprise me—He answered my question! Not audibly, but in that "still, small voice" that emanates from within, I heard a statement that I knew didn't come from myself.

"Listen to your heart!"

The thought startled me. Listen to my heart? What did that mean? Then I remembered one of my favorite scripture verses, "Delight yourself in the Lord; and He will give you the desires of your heart" (Psalm 37:4). Could it be that I had just admitted that being at home full-time was my heart's desire?

I had spent the earliest years of my marriage at home, feeling that our children needed a mother during their formative years more than we needed extra income. When they started attending school I began working outside the home, mostly on a part-time basis. But now I was working more and enjoying it less. I no longer had the time or the energy to do the things at home that I felt were important, and it left me feeling very unfulfilled.

Then that inner voice spoke again.

"Why do you think you are happiest when you are in your own home? Why do you think that you are most content when you're working there? Don't you realize that your contentment comes from Me? I put it in you Myself! Don't think it's something wrong with you—it's something right with you to be most satisfied when you are in your own home."

Suddenly I realized that my deep-seated love of taking care of my family and my home was, indeed, a desire that God Himself had deposited in my heart. Thinking about that made all the pieces fit together—the great sense of security and contentment that I always drew from working in my home came from being where God had created me to fit the best. When I was happy and secure, I was able to create a serene, tranquil atmosphere inside my home. That, in turn, made our home a welcome refuge for my husband and children when they returned there from a busy, tiring, or stressful day.

When I, too, came home after an exhausting day at work, no one was ever there to minister peace and healing to any of us. That's why God was encouraging me to make our home a haven for us. I could function as the "footwasher," much like Jesus washed the feet of His disciples, cleansing them of the dust they had picked up while walking through a dirty world.

I also began to see the wisdom of Paul's words, telling women to be "workers at home," or as the King James Version puts it, "keepers at home" (Titus 2:5). Perhaps this command was as inspired as the rest of the Bible, and not just some cultural standard of Paul's day. Perhaps it was written not only for the benefit of the family, but also for the benefit of the woman herself.

As I pondered those things in my heart, I also began an informal survey of my female co-workers. Not knowing how to tactfully introduce the subject, I just bluntly asked, "If money was not a factor and you could do anything you wanted to do, would you continue in your job or would you prefer to stay home?"

I was startled by their candidness. The overwhelming majority responded with an immediate, "I would stay home in a minute!" Most of them also said, "I like my job, and I derive some satisfaction from it. But I would love more than anything to stay home." Rare was the woman who said, "Oh, I'd be too bored. I would rather go to work every day than stay home." But there were a few for whom boredom was a real fear. I knew from personal experience that boredom was never a problem for me—I could always think of endless ways to keep myself occupied at home, even more than at a paying job!

One woman, who had to enter the work force after a divorce, impressed me with how deeply the home itself ministers peace and security to a woman's heart. She said, "When I first started working, I missed my home so much that every day I spent my thirty minute lunch break just going home. It took me ten minutes to drive there, and ten minutes to drive back to work, which only gave me ten minutes to be home. That didn't even allow me time to eat, but I didn't care. It just felt so good to sit there for ten minutes! It helped me get through the rest of the day. If I still worked that close to home, I would still be doing it today. After all these years of having to support myself, I miss being a homemaker more than anything."

Economics seemed to be the major obstacle for most women. So many women were divorced, most with children to support, and they had no choice about working outside the home. Few such women are fortunate to have home-based paying careers. Many women were married, but found their husband's income inadequate to support their family. There were also many women, like myself, who worked simply to augment the family income. It might be a sacrifice to do without the extras that job provided, but with some effort it could be done.

When I approached my husband with the idea of my staying home full-time, I was surprised by his response. "That's fine with me. By the time you subtract taxes and expenses from your paycheck, it's hardly worth all the inconvenience it causes the whole family." I was free!

This book is written for every woman who has been blessed with the freedom to leave the business world behind and become a "homebody"—someone whose life centers on the home. Today books and magazines are glutted with advice for the "working woman" (every woman is a working woman!) on how to survive at home. Although much of the information in this book would be helpful to those with full-time jobs, this book is written for the homemaker who wants to go beyond surviving—to thriving!

1

What is a Homemaker?

It's an exuberant spring day, and I'm knee deep in the process of transplanting lilies in our back yard. My hair is askew, my sweatshirt is sweaty, and my tennis shoes are caked with mud as I labor at digging another hole. In short, I am enjoying myself immensely.

Then my neighbor Ted approaches with clippers in hand and leans over the hedge. "Hello, neighbor! How did you all survive the winter?"

"Just great!" I reply, feeling as sunny as the moment.

"So how is the health care business going?"

"Oh, didn't you know? I quit that job."

"Gone back to nursing instead?" Ted asks as he mops his brow. My mind flashes back to the day Ted boasted about his wife receiving an award for five years at work without missing a day, and I wish he would drop the whole subject. I begin digging harder.

"Nope."

"Well, then, you must be selling real estate again."

"Nope," I repeat, digging furiously.

"Oh." (Pregnant pause.) "Just what are you doing with yourself these days?"

I wish I could throw Ted into this hole and quickly cover it over. I visualize myself jumping up and down on top of the mound of dirt as he muffles, "You're doing what?" Ted waits persistently for my answer. I shrug my shoulders and nervously giggle, "Oh, I'm just a housewife!"

Ted assumes a quizzical expression and mumbles something inane like, "Oh . . . how interesting," before disappearing behind the shrubs. I resist the urge to lob a dirt clod at the back of his head. Suddenly the sky seems overcast, and I retreat to the hammock to berate myself.

What's the matter with me, anyway? Why do I feel so defensive every time someone asks me what I "do"? Ever since I decided to be a full-time homemaker, it's as if I'm afraid that others think I no longer qualify as a productive member of society. And why on earth did I say, "I'm just a housewife"? I hate that expression!

Gardening forgotten, I gaze listlessly at the oak trees towering overhead and wonder what would be a good answer the next time someone asks me what I "do" now. Just what, exactly, is a homemaker anyway? I ask myself. I promptly decide that a homemaker is definitely not "just a housewife." That expression is so condescending—as if it is something one does only if she is incapable of doing anything else. It sounds like "just breathing" or "just hanging around, doing nothing." And I don't like the word "housewife." It sounds like someone married to her house. Yes, I decide, "homemaker" is a much better word than "housewife."

But just what is a homemaker?

She obviously is not considered by most people to be a career woman, even if homemaking is definitely her career of choice. And she hasn't the prestige of dashing off to her "liberated career in the economic-opportunity sphere," the status of an impressive title, nor even the reward of receiving a paycheck at the end of the week.

But the homemaker does have the satisfaction of knowing that what she does is much more valuable than any of those things—and it's far more rewarding in the long run. And she feels very important, even if her "status" is only appreciated by her family.

The career homemaker is also liberated—much more than any women's lib activists give her credit for. She's relieved to be liberated from angry, unfeminine "feminism"—free to be as caring, nurturing, and gentle as she may wish to be. She is thankful to be liberated from the tyranny of the time clock, demands from department heads, and the time pressures of trying to handle a forty hour a week job besides the jobs that never go away when one is a wife and mother. This sets her free to be her own boss, to schedule her own time, and to sleep late or take the day off if she wishes.

The homemaker is also liberated from the no-win situations that inevitably arise from trying to force a husband and children to do the tasks of a wife and mother. She knows that not even AT&T could survive if the company president, the accountants, the secretaries, the janitors, and all the other employees were forced to do "their share" of everyone else's work. Every successful institution knows there is good reason for clear divisions of labor and definite job descriptions. The homemaker is happy to function solely in her role as wife, mother, and home manager. This frees her husband to concentrate fully on providing for his family. And it saves their children from forced, premature adulthood so they can "just be kids." When their youngsters do grow up, they will be prepared to function as mature adults rather than overgrown, unfulfilled children. Yes, the homemaker and her family are very liberated. Perhaps that's why America has fourteen million women still at home full-time,[1] and seventy percent of married mothers do not work full-time all year.[2]

What is a homemaker? She is not, as many would have us believe, a relic of a bygone era, a Wilma Flintstone, nor even a June Cleaver. Nor is she a wealthy yuppie who idles away the hours while the maid does all the work. Her husband can be the king of his castle because that makes her the queen. She is content to be her husband's "helpmeet," as well as his cheerleader, his comforter, and his ally. She does not compete with her husband, but complements him. Even though they may in many ways be opposites, together they function as one.

In this day of two-paycheck families, she appreciates having a husband who supports her stay-at-home career. He, in turn, is thankful to have a wife who chooses to make homemaking her primary, rather than secondary, concern. He knows that after expenses incurred from child care, transportation, work-related clothes, and eating out, the average American woman nets roughly $2.30 per hour.[3]

He considers a more frugal lifestyle well worth the true higher standard of living his family enjoys as the result of having a wife dedicated to managing their home lovingly, wisely, and more economically. Most of all, he enjoys having a wife who has the time and energy to devote to being his friend and lover.

The career homemaker and her husband are not easily fooled into believing the false truisms that are accepted without question by society, such as, "You just can't live on one paycheck anymore," and "Families can't afford to have women in the home like they did in the good old days of our parents."

They know that, according to Census Bureau statistics, the typical American family's income was 50 percent higher in 1986 as it was in 1960, and that the average American commands twice as much buying power today as in 1952, when our mothers stayed home.[4] And, despite the rhetoric, she knows that even in homes with a full-time homemaker, today's breadwinner brings home an average of 34 percent more income than our parents did.

They also know that most of us today are just not content to live as simply as our parents did. Compare the size of our homes and closets, the options on our cars, and our staggering credit card debt. If the homemaker must choose between the pursuit of yuppie materialism or the pursuit of a homemaking career, the homemaker agrees that "godliness actually is a means of great gain, when accompanied by contentment" (1 Timothy 6:6). Or as Euripides put it, "Enough is abundance to the wise."

The homemaker does not, however, judge those who feel otherwise. She has sincere concern for those women who have no other recourse than an outside-the-home job. She has no desire to add to their burden with criticism. Instead, she often cares for their children and offers a kind hand wherever she can help. The career homemaker is also a devoted mother. Whether her children are very young or have left the nest, they know that Mom is always there for them at a moment's notice.

The homemaker never ceases to be a mother. At various stages of her life, her kids may ask, "Mommy, did I tell you that I have to be a frog in the school play tomorrow?" or "Mama, do you think I have a fever?" or "Hey, Mom, we can't find a babysitter—what are you doing Saturday night?" She enjoys listening to, caring for, and serving her children. She will never have to say, like actress Roseanne Barr, "I'm the mother they never had."[5]

Unlike society, which has come to regard children as necessary evils, the homemaker considers her children to be her greatest treasures, and she endeavors to raise them accordingly. She doesn't entrust their upbringing to the school, the state, or to surrogate mothers. She is grateful not to have to, and she certainly doesn't choose to. As a result, her children benefit from enjoying not only quality time but quantity time with their mother.

The career homemaker does not concern herself with whether or not her duties are all "fun." She doesn't kid herself: changing diapers and cleaning toilets is not all laughs. But she understands that fun does not equal happiness. She knows that fun is the feeling one derives from an enjoyable act, like gliding down a water slide or floating along in a hot air balloon. But happiness is the feeling one has between all those few and fleeting fun moments. If fun could make a person happy, she concludes, then why is the world full of so many laughing, partying, fun-loving people who are living empty, miserable lives?

According to one writer, society applies the maxim "No pain, no gain" to the physical conditioning of our bodies but, mistakenly, not to life.[6] The homemaker knows that everything capable of bringing real happiness must, at times, also be painful. She considers marriage, childbirth, motherhood, spiritual growth, and homemaking all to be pursuits worthy of their cost. She doesn't expect every moment to be fun, but she does expect her efforts to bring happiness—and they do.

A homemaker is also a very flexible person. She must function under pressure in an overwhelming variety of roles: chauffeur, nutritionist, nurse, counselor, teacher, social secretary, financial director, interior decorator, savvy bargain hunter, holiday planner and entertainer, good neighbor and informed citizen, church volunteer, Scout leader, and disaster relief worker. She attempts to do all that and more with an air of grace, always striving to be the best person that she can be in the process. No one is harder on her than herself when she fails. Thankfully, the homemaker is also resilient.

The career homemaker knows that the only way that she can accomplish the many demands made on her is to be an excellent organizer and time manager. If she "just can't get everything done" and is suffering pressure from time constraints, her anxiety may be caused by two things. First, she may not be using her time wisely. Second, she may be suffering from the "Supermom Syndrome"—trying to be all things to all people. Ninety percent of the time her frustration stems from the latter cause!

To avoid these problems the homemaker does several things. First, she starts her day with a "quiet time" in which she asks for God's guidance and wisdom for that day. She knows that He will not give her more things to do in one day than she has the hours in which to do them. She does not over-schedule her time, but she allows God the freedom to add to or delete from her schedule as He chooses. And she does not create self-imposed guilt by setting higher standards for herself than God has asked her to set. She lives her life according to the Bible, not *Better Homes & Gardens.*

Second, the homemaker strives to be organized. She schedules her time; she organizes her home for greater efficiency; and she eliminates the non-essentials. In her personal life, as well as in her home, she considers clutter to be her greatest enemy and simplicity to be her greatest friend.

The successful homemaker cannot afford to waste time. She considers her time on this earth to be a finite gift from God, and she does not squander it on soap operas, trashy romance novels, or long telephone gossip sessions. She does not say yes to anything she is not absolutely sure she should do. And she feels that if she has time for tennis, bridge, garden club, or even church activities but does not have time to manage her home wisely, her priorities are out of order.

The homemaker does not waste time so that she can allow time for activities that are important to her. She considers time spent on herself, relaxing and enjoying her solitary company, to be time well spent. She insists on having time with her husband and with her children. And she enjoys having time to practice the nearly extinct art of hospitality. She knows that the only way she can enjoy these pleasant activities is to guard her time and manage it wisely.

A Christian homemaker also honors the Word of God. Scripture tells her that "older women likewise are to . . . encourage the young women to love their husbands, to love their children, to be sensible, pure, workers at home . . . that the word of God may not be dishonored" (Titus 2:3-5). As a sincere disciple of Christ, she does not consider obedience to the Word of God to be an option.

She seeks to pattern herself after the godly women throughout the Scriptures, such as the excellent wife described in Proverbs 31:10-31. Like that homemaker, she strives to be productive, kind, wise, and such a blessing to her husband and children that they have "no lack of gain" because of her constant efforts on their behalf.

But, most of all, the homemaker attempts to pattern herself after Jesus Himself, who embodied what it means to be a servant, comforter, healer, peacemaker, teacher, lover of little children, and a giver of life. All that she does, no matter how seemingly insignificant, she does for Jesus. And she strives to do all things as Jesus does them—motivated by love, in perfect order, and with grace and beauty.

Brother Lawrence, the humble seventeenth century monk, was happy just to pick up a straw from the ground for the love of God. In that same way, the homemaker is pleased to do the humblest of tasks. Whether she is making a bed or wiping a little nose, when she remembers for Whom she is really doing it, she derives a great sense of joy and purpose.

What is a homemaker? In short, *she is a person who makes a home.* To her, a home must be more than a motel and fast-food stop. Just as she recognizes that the family is the strength of a nation, she knows that the home is the strength of the family. She strives to make her home a place of beauty, order, and security—a positive retreat from a negative and turbulent world. There her family finds the healing and refreshing they need to face that world anew each day. There they are built up, rather than beaten down. There they can be open and vulnerable, knowing they are loved unconditionally.

That is the home this homemaker strives to create, realizing that she has the important role of mood setter and atmosphere-maker for her home. If she is having a "down" day, it casts a shadow on everyone else. If she is "up," soon everyone else feels better, too.

The homemaker strives to make her home a garden where love can grow between her and her husband, free of the weeds of contention and criticism. Her home is a greenhouse for tender, growing children. And she is the gardener.

That, I decide, is what a homemaker is. Then I pick up my shovel and begin to plant lilies.

2

Never Clean for Company

"Sometimes I think about just quitting my job and staying home," my friend Evelyn confided over lunch. "I get tired of the same old nine-to-five routine. I can afford to quit if I really want to. But when I get right down to doing it, I lose my nerve. You see," she added pensively, "I'm just not the type to stay home and clean house all day."

Many women consider homemaking to be synonymous with only one thing—cleaning the house. No wonder so many women are reluctant to be full-time homemakers. They have entered the job market by the droves because even the hassles of a job look glamorous compared to keeping company with Mr. Tidybowl. And if cleaning house is all there is to homemaking, who can blame them?

That's how Jacky felt, too. Despite having three active children, a beautiful house, and a husband who provided well for the family, she was dissatisfied with her life at home.

"I'm too intelligent to waste my life behind a mop and broom," she complained. "I hate housework. I'm not good at it, either. I'd rather do anything else."

So Jacky got a job. And who does the housework in Jacky's home now? Her husband does. And when does he do all that housework? On Saturdays. Jacky abandoned homemaking to escape doing what her husband accomplishes on his day off. It makes me wonder.

I also wonder about people like Pat. She's a full-time homemaker who makes herself miserable over housework. She never seems to get caught up. Whenever you go to her house, she makes you uncomfortable by apologizing profusely for "this awful mess." She acts as if you came to inspect her house, not to enjoy her company. She seems to be in constant anguish over what she thinks is an insurmountable task—getting the house clean.

Pat has an especially hard time whenever she is expecting houseguests. She works herself into a frenzy, trying to accomplish in one day what hasn't been done in months. By the time her guests arrive, Pat is too exhausted to be much of a hostess. She simply horrifies them by looking so haggard and telling them how very hard she worked to prepare for their visit. Her guests undoubtedly feel sorry that they came. It's a no-win situation.

If only Pat knew that she should never clean for company. It really shouldn't be necessary. With just a little organization and discipline, Pat could make sure her house looks good enough for company all the time. No extra fuss. No last minute panic. Pat could invest all that wasted energy she spends on worry, rationalization, and procrastination on one weekly cleaning session of only four hours or less. And she could maintain that clean appearance in only thirty minutes a day. The rest of her week would be free to pursue other interests.

If only Pat, Jacky, and Evelyn understood that homemaking is much more than just cleaning the house, perhaps they would begin to enjoy the great rewards of a full-time homemaking career. Of course, homemaking includes housework. Cleanliness is a basic necessity for every home, and no amount of fancy decorating can hide dirt. The successful homemaker must first provide a clean environment.

Some women act like cleaning is a dirty word. But housework, if done in an organized manner, need not be terribly time consuming. And it need not be a task that takes all the joy out of homemaking. Housework is one of those areas where an ounce of prevention is worth a pound of cure. A weekly cleaning routine keeps the work from piling up into an overwhelming chore. And a daily touch-up session keeps the house looking fresh all week.

How to Clean Like a Pro

I, too, used to spend far too much time cleaning the house. But when our sons started school, I got a job and no longer had time for all that housework. So I hired a housekeeper. She came once a week, and she was expensive. But she was worth it. I looked forward to coming home once a week to a sparkling, orderly house. It was such a luxury to know that someone had done all those hours of housework for me.

Then one summer I learned from the boys just how much time my housekeeper spent doing "all those hours of housework." Only two hours! I couldn't believe it! I had them time her the next week, and the next. But she consistently accomplished in only two hours what it had always taken me much longer to do. This startling revelation led me to ask myself three serious questions:

1. How could she clean my house in only two hours?
2. If she could clean my house in only two hours, why couldn't I?
3. If I could clean my house in only two hours, why was I paying her to do it?

That's when I decided to revolutionize my method of cleaning the house. I decided to stop cleaning like I had all week to do it and start cleaning like a professional. A professional cleans as quickly and efficiently as possible, treating housework like a business, not a hobby. So my goal became doing the best job in the least amount of time. But, for the sake of doing a good job without unnecessary time pressure, I decided to allow myself twice as much time as my housekeeper took—four hours.

Then I broke down my housework duties into just four categories:

1. Dusting
2. Vacuuming
3. Cleaning the kitchen
4. Cleaning the bathrooms

This allowed me one hour to do each of these four jobs. But could I do it? After my first trial run I learned it was not only possible, but easy. Here's how you can do it, too.

Choose one morning or afternoon per week for your housework, and stick to that schedule if possible. Write it on your calendar so you won't inadvertently plan something else during that time. Make it a weekly appointment, and soon it will become a regular habit.

I like to clean the house early in the week. Weekends are the messiest time of the week, so a good cleaning early in the week seems to last longer than if I cleaned on Friday. I would never clean on Friday anyway because I want to be rested and ready to go out or have guests. Make it a rule never to clean on the same day you're having company!

If this four-hour schedule is too rugged for you, or small children make it impossible to have a four-hour uninterrupted block of time, simply set up the schedule any way you want it. Maybe you would prefer to spend two hours dusting and vacuuming on Monday and another two hours on the baths and kitchen on Thursday. Or perhaps you would do better to work one hour a day on Tuesday through Friday. For example, you could leave Mondays for the laundry and ironing, Tuesdays for the kitchen, Wednesdays for the bathrooms, Thursdays for the dusting, and Fridays for vacuuming the carpets. This prevents you from being overwhelmed by having to do more than one housecleaning task per day.

My friend Barb said, "That's fine if you don't have preschoolers at home, but I do. There's just too much constant clutter all over the house from the children for me to make any headway on cleaning."

I suggested that Barb try the solution that I found to that problem when my boys were home all day. I removed all the toys from their bedrooms except for their stuffed animals and books. The toys went down to our unfinished basement where I put them in toyboxes and on shelves. There they had plenty of room to ride their tricycles and run off steam on cold or rainy days, and an area rug on which to sit and scatter toys to their hearts' delight. But if they wanted to play with their toys upstairs, they were allowed to bring up only one thing at a time, and it had to be taken back downstairs before they could bring up another toy. It worked wonderfully, allowing the children the freedom to make their own choices in what they wanted to do while teaching them to pick up after themselves, too.

Another alternative would be to work out a babysitting exchange with a neighbor: you watch her children while she cleans her house if she will keep your children while you clean yours. It's well worth the effort of setting up a schedule to allow the rest of your week to be free from worrying about housework.

A word of caution: The following simple tips can revolutionize your life. You'll never again have to fear an unexpected knock at the door. Company will always be welcome. You will know that your work is done, eliminating energy-sapping worry and guilt. Your time and energy will be free for more important and enjoyable things.

But, on the other hand, your new housework schedule must not become too important. If family or friends need you, of course, your schedule must have some flexibility. (Just be sure you aren't using those opportunities for service to avoid your household tasks.) If you don't get everything done on schedule this week, there's always next week. This schedule, however you decide to set it up, is designed to free you—not to be master over you.

Take care not to turn your home into a showroom unfit for human occupation. Your home, after all, is also your family's home—and they should feel comfortable there. Nobody else cares if your two-year-old has Potato People scattered all over the family room floor, so why should you? And it's better to have several messy teenagers sprawled all over your house than who-knows-where-else.

If someone comes over in the midst of a bit of people-clutter like that, be confident enough not to apologize for the mess. This avoids the old arguments, "Oh, it's not half as bad as my house," and "No, your house is always cleaner than mine." Just allow your guest to feel at ease because you are, whatever the state of your house. This is an important element to being a gracious hostess.

Being organized and capable of cleaning your house in four hours or less does not eliminate the need to teach your children how to do these things, which is certainly a more difficult task. Daughters should be taught how to do housework so that they will one day be capable of taking care of their own families. Sons should be taught how to do housework so they'll not get married just because they don't know how to take care of themselves. Homemaking skills should be taught to children so they gradually gain self-sufficiency—not so they do our work for us. Heaven knows, it's easier to do it yourself!

Here's an example of a four-hour Tuesday morning schedule:

8:00-9:00 a.m.   Dusting
9:00-10:00 a.m. Vacuuming

> 10:00-11:00 a.m.   Cleaning the kitchen
> 11:00-noon   Cleaning the bathrooms

Let's look at each cleaning segment in more detail.

Dusting

You may wonder, "Why should I dust first? Won't I just stir up more dust when I vacuum?" You dust first for two reasons: First, dusting often knocks little bits of debris onto the carpeting. Second, many people have plush carpeting that shows footprints, so they prefer not to vacuum first and then track footprints all over the carpeting when dusting.

Vacuuming after you dust will not stir up dust if you take the following precautions. First, change your furnace filter once a month to keep dust out of the air circulation. I spray my filter with a no-wax dusting spray to help it collect dust better. Keep a record of your filter size in your purse notebook (see Chapter 7) so you don't pick up the wrong size at the store. Buy a box of a dozen filters at a time, and you'll only have to purchase them once a year. Second, if you consistently clean your house once a week, it will gradually have less and less dust in it. I know one woman who says she needs to dust only once a month. Her house must really be clean! If regular cleaning doesn't help, you may need a furnace cleaning service to power-vac your ventilation ducts.

Starting at one end of the house, systematically dust one room at a time thoroughly. Dust from the top of the room to the bottom, from one side to the other. Put away misplaced items and straighten the room as you work. Pick up items rather than dusting around them. Use spray dusting liquid and a clean rag on flat surfaces and fingerprinted areas. If you carry along a small bucket with a damp rag and all-purpose spray cleaner, you can swipe fingerprints from doors and woodwork as you go.

Purchasing a duster on a handle is well worth the investment. Mine is eighteen inches long, half of which is covered with lamb's wool, which attracts rather than scatters dust. You can use your duster to reach everything from ceiling fixtures to the baseboards. Use it to dust intricately carved crevices, caned chairs, window sills, and mini-blinds. Run it across your clean air return vents to keep dust from collecting there. A duster on a handle makes dusting much easier, faster, and more thorough. Just shake it outdoors to remove collected dust before you go on to the next room.

Many women complain that housework is "no brain" work, making it monotonous and boring. So they turn on the TV and get hooked on soap operas or other non-productive programs. Why not use your housework time productively instead? You could listen to tapes that are inspiring, educational, or uplifting. Use a portable cassette player with headphones if you don't want to disturb other family members who may be home. Most libraries carry audiotapes of classic books that you might otherwise never have the time to read. They also carry classical music that you can use to learn all about the works of Beethoven or Handel. Many church libraries have the Bible on tape. I especially like to listen to Christian teaching tapes. I get so involved in some of them that I finish my housework before I'm ready to stop listening. If I want to work quickly, I put on an upbeat worship tape and dance through my work.

But probably the greatest use of your housecleaning time is to pray while you work. Have you ever complained that you just don't have enough time for prayer? If so, here's a great four-hour slot that can be used for that purpose. While your body is doing the physical work, your spirit can petition God for your needs, engage in spiritual warfare, or just lift up heavenly praises. If you use your time like that, you won't ever again complain that housework is boring. If you finish a particular job in less than an hour, put your feet up for a few minutes while you sip a glass of juice or a cup of tea. Make your work more fun by learning to give yourself little goals and rewards throughout the day.

Vacuuming

During this hour you not only vacuum all the carpeting, but also clean any floors other than those in the kitchen and bathrooms. You may need to dustmop the entry hall or your screened-in porch. Shake out the area throw rugs while you're at it.

Be kind enough to yourself to own a decent vacuum sweeper. Too often women exhaust themselves by pushing around a cheap imitation of a real sweeper because they're too frugal to invest in an effective cleaning machine. Men, however, rarely suffer from this particular martyr behavior. If they need a saw or a drill, they usually buy the deluxe model—even if they only need to use it once a year. How many men have elaborate carpentry machinery collecting cobwebs in their basements while their wives struggle upstairs behind a worn out, twenty-year-old sweeper?

Once my friend Kim was vigorously pulling her old canister sweeper behind her and wondered why her little boy began to scream, "Moke! Moke!" as he excitedly pointed at the sweeper. She turned around to see that it was on fire!

So don't skimp on having a safe, powerful upright sweeper with a beater bar that does the work for you, instead of making you do it. Today they aren't very expensive, and they even save you money by cleaning your carpeting better and prolonging its life.

Sweep systematically and thoroughly from one room to the next. Don't wear yourself out by trying to sweep under every piece of furniture every week—nobody but the cat walks under there anyway. Just concentrate on doing an extra thorough job on a different room each week, and you'll never be overwhelmed by needing to do it all at once.

If you have a convenient place to store one, it's also nice to have a little hand vac to pull out for crumbs and tracked spots during the week. It's a lot easier than lugging out a big sweeper for a little job.

Cleaning the Kitchen

Shake out throw rugs and set them aside. Dustmop the floor to remove loose debris. Then mop the floor with a weak solution of ammonia in water. At least once a month mop the floor by hand. (No, I'm not kidding!) Instead of doing a good job, sponge mopping pushes dirt into corners and crevices. When you clean the floors by hand, you can get all that dirt and wipe off the woodwork at the same time. Just use a gardener's foam kneepad, fix a bucket of weak ammonia-water, and get it over with before you can talk yourself out of it. I do my kitchen, breakfast room, and laundry room in under thirty minutes. Really.

Once the floor is clean, fill the sink with ammonia-water and wipe off all the countertops and appliances. Soak dirty stove drip pans in the water while you work, then wash them off and replace them. Get as much clutter off the countertops and top of the refrigerator as possible. Too many magnets and clippings on the front of the refrigerator can make the whole kitchen look messy. If you have a lot of paper clutter, put up a bulletin board. When you're finished, just replace the rugs and put an attractive centerpiece on the table. The kitchen looks great!

Cleaning the Bathrooms

You can clean a bathroom in approximately twenty to thirty minutes, allowing you to clean two or three bathrooms in an hour. Remove everything that you can from the bathroom and place it all on a throw rug or towel on the floor outside the bathroom. You don't want to be cleaning around soap dishes and knick-knacks.

In a plastic bucket, basket, or wastebasket, make a bathroom cleaning kit consisting of a can of your favorite cleanser, a spray bottle of window cleaner, rubber gloves, and clean rags. Anything other than that is probably not

necessary—including cute little plastic mushroom deodorizers and blue toilet water dyes. All your bathroom needs
to look and smell great is a good cleaning and a fat cake of
fresh soap in the soap dish. Don't be fooled into buying lots
of expensive cleansers and deodorizers that you don't need.
You can spend that money on scented soaps or luxurious
bubblebath if you want.

Clean bath fixtures in the following order: sink, tub, toilet, and floor. Using a clean rag, rinse bath fixtures in the
same order. This prevents spreading bacterial contamination
from dirty areas to less dirty areas. To make rinsing the
shower and tub walls easier, you may want to install a
showerhead on a hose. You'll eliminate the "drippy elbow
syndrome" forever.

Clean the mirror and polish the chrome fixtures to a shine
with window spray. Then shake out the throw rugs, empty
the wastebasket, and throw dirty towels in the washing
machine. Return everything to its place, and you're done.

Now fill up the tub with some warm water, pour in some
of that scented bubblebath that you bought, and jump in
for a long soak. It's only noon, and your whole house is
clean for the week! Once you get your four-hour routine
down to a science, you may want to start by stripping the
beds and keeping the washer and dryer running while you
work. You can have all the bedding and towels washed and
back in place by the time your work is done.

Daily Maintenance

No house is going to stay spotless all week if it has people living in it, so a little daily maintenance is necessary.
That's why a thirty-minute touch-up session every morning means the difference between a house that looks like
you cleaned it recently and a house that looks like you
cleaned it today. Plan your touch-up session after the family
has left for work and school, and after you've gotten dressed

for the day. It's important to do this every morning. Once it becomes a daily habit you won't know how you ever lived any other way.

1. Make your bed. My friend Kathy used to think that she didn't have time to make her bed on very rushed days. Then one day she timed herself. It took just three minutes. Now she knows that she can always spare three minutes to make her bed. Straighten your bedroom, putting away clothes, books, etc. Open the curtains and let the sunshine in.

2. Check each child's room. Teach them to make their own beds and put away their own clothes and toys. Supervise the little ones pleasantly so they will have a positive attitude about caring for their own room.

3. Straighten the bathrooms. Throw dirty towels in the hamper and close the shower curtain to prevent mildew. Keep a bottle of window cleaner under the sink so you can spray and wipe the mirror and vanity top. The bathroom will look and smell like you just cleaned the whole room. This is probably the single most important worksaver you can perform. Try it!

4. Walk through the remaining rooms of the house. As you go through each one, straighten and put away clutter. You may want to carry a plastic basket with you for carrying things from one room to the next. This takes very little time, but makes an enormous difference.

5. Straighten the kitchen last. Put away dishes and wipe off countertops and table. Pull from the freezer whatever you plan to cook for dinner, or get the crockpot going if you plan to be away all day. If you're the only one home during the day, you may want to set the dinner table now, saving yourself precious moments at the hectic dinner hour. You'll thank yourself at 5:00 p.m. for everything you do now.

6. Throw a load of clothes in the washing machine and turn it on. You can throw them in the dryer at dinnertime and fold them after doing the dishes. Doing a load a day like this keeps laundry day from becoming a nightmare.

Keeping this touch-up routine as a daily habit is the greatest secret to being an organized, efficient housekeeper. For the few minutes a day it requires, it's more than worth the freedom and self-esteem it pays in return. Soon you'll find your friends asking you how on earth you do it all. You can even tell them your secret if you want to. But you don't have to.

Action Assignments

1. Time how long it takes you to make your bed.
2. Time how long it takes you to do each of the four categories of housecleaning: dusting, vacuuming, bathrooms, and kitchen.
3. Assign yourself a time to do your weekly housecleaning and write it on your calendar. See if you can accomplish it in four hours or less—and in the time slot that you scheduled.
4. Plan what mentally productive thing you will do while cleaning your house (such as listening to tapes or praying). See if you feel that it makes your work more enjoyable.
5. Make a cleaning kit to keep in one of your bathrooms for your weekly cleaning. Put a pair of rubber gloves, a can of cleanser, a bottle of window spray cleaner, and some clean rags in a plastic bucket or other container. Put another bottle of window spray in each of your other bathrooms for the thirty-minute daily touch-up.
6. Make a note on your calendar to change your furnace/air conditioner filter once a month. Make note of your filter size in your datebook (see Chapter 7) and buy a box of twelve on your next shopping day.

3

No More Spring Cleaning

Our grandmothers had an annual ritual that came as surely as crocus, daffodils, and little green apples. They called it "spring cleaning"—that wildly disruptive time of year when all other activities ceased so that everything could be cleaned that hadn't been cleaned since the year before. Families fled for the outdoors to escape the commotion as Grandma furiously shook out carpets, washed windows, and scrubbed everything else to a spit shine. In the process Grandma also wore herself to a frazzle. Fortunately, spring cleaning only came once a year—and Grandma needed that long to rest up from it.

Today not many women have the time and energy to invest in an annual spring cleaning. We have schedules far too crammed full of carpooling, shopping, and going to Little League games to allow us a couple of weeks devoted exclusively to deep-cleaning our homes every spring.

So what happens to our homes if they never get the benefit of that old-fashioned spring cleaning? Do we try, unsuccessfully and halfheartedly, to fit it in here and there? Do we decide to ignore the gray fuzz on the top edge of the drapes until next year? Do we search the Yellow Pages for someone who advertises, "We do windows, wash and iron curtains, and pick the grit out of your sliding glass door tracks"? (Lotsa luck!) Or do we just forget about it until it's our turn to have the family over for Thanksgiving—and we find ourselves polishing the silver, ironing the good table-cloth, and cleaning out the china cabinet while trying to make the turkey and dressing? What else can a busy homemaker do?

The best method I've found to keep my home in decent condition while avoiding a yearly "spring cleaning" is simple—just do the work in smaller bits throughout the year. Instead of consolidating all your deep cleaning into one or two exhausting weeks, break the work down into twelve segments—one segment for each month of the year.

For example, perhaps you would like to "spring clean" each room of the house once a year. Assign a room or special activity for each month of the year. A once-a-year deep cleaning is usually adequate for most areas if you practice the regular housecleaning described in Chapter 2. You may want to leave the month of December free of heavy house-work and devote it to baking cookies, mailing Christmas cards, and doing last-minute shopping. On a piece of paper list your monthly special projects. When you finish, your list may look something like this:

January:	Basement or attic
February:	Office and files
March:	Kitchen
April:	Master bedroom and closet
May:	Bedroom #2
June:	Bedroom #3
July:	Family room
August:	Laundry room
September:	Bathroom and linen closet
October:	Living room, entry hall, and coat closet

November: Dining room
December: Christmas activities

"But when during the month do I do all this cleaning?" you ask. One option is to spend some extra time on that particular area during your weekly cleaning routine. If it's the month to clean your bedroom, you might wash the curtains and clean the windows one week, clean out your closet and dresser drawers the next week, the third week you can wash the mattress pad and turn the mattress, and the last week of the month you could wipe down the walls and woodwork. You do as much of those extra things as you want to do each week. At the beginning of the next month, you start doing the same type of thing on the next project. Adding this extra work on the same day that you clean the whole house can be tiring, but this system works if that's the only time you can devote to it. And it's still easier than trying to do it all at one time of the year.

Another option, which I prefer, is to schedule yourself a Special Projects Day each week. Perhaps you choose Thursday mornings. That's your morning to do all the "spring cleaning" you want on your monthly project. If you don't finish that week, you follow up with more work the next week, and the next, until you've accomplished all you want to on that particular project. This method gives me time to do a much more thorough job. I can even tackle extra fixing-up or decorating projects on that room as well.

Sometimes I get my monthly Special Project done in one morning, and sometimes it takes "a month of Thursdays." Sometimes the room just needs a good cleaning. Other times I may decide to paint the woodwork, paper the walls, or rearrange all the furniture. Regardless of how much or how little I do, *my goal is to feel good about that room at the end of the month.*

Keep in mind that Special Projects Day is your once-a-year opportunity to take a good, hard look at each room and reassess its appearance and function. Look at that room as if you were a guest seeing it for the first time. We can get so accustomed to our surroundings that we no longer realize how they look to others. We may not notice the little fingerprints accumulating on the door frames. We may not see that the sofa needs a good upholstery scrubbing. Maybe the kitchen curtain over the sink has grown faded and worn. Perhaps you never noticed that heavy traffic is wearing a path in the carpeting in front of the sofa. Use this time to view your home through a more critical eye.

It's amazing how we can overlook the obvious through habit. When I sold real estate, our office took weekly tours of pre-owned homes that had just been placed on the market. Some of the homes were very attractive and well-maintained. But most of those homes were, at best, dull and neglected. Some were even disgraceful. I wondered if the people trying to sell their homes ever really looked at what they had grown accustomed to living in.

After I put someone's home on the market, the owners often began to hurriedly "fix it up" to attract a buyer. They rushed to paint, repair, and replace things that had needed their attention for years. Now that they were moving out of the house, they were getting all that done. But they could have enjoyed the fruits of their own efforts had they only done it when their home first needed repair. Now they were doing it for someone else—and doing it under pressure. What a waste!

Remember that nothing you do to keep your home well-maintained is a waste. It always adds to the value of your home and to your present enjoyment of it. Your home is probably your most valuable investment, so it doesn't pay to neglect it. Having a Special Projects routine is one way to be sure your home is always in excellent condition and "market ready" if you should suddenly need to move.

Here are some suggestions for your Special Projects activities:

Suggestions for Every Room

1. Write down projects that you need to do or items that you need to buy. As you work you may notice that you need more hangers, shelf paper, or plastic crates for organizing small items. If you don't write it down when you think of it, you probably won't remember it when you go to the store.

2. Repair anything that is broken. Tighten wiggly doorknobs and switch plates. (Yes, you can do this yourself!) Reglue curling edges of wallpaper. Put plastic wallpaper guards on corners to prevent wear. Replace burned-out light bulbs and wash light fixtures. Clean or replace dirty lamp shades. Have damaged windows or screens repaired. Touch up wooden furniture with scratch remover.

3. Clean windows and window treatments. Take draperies to the cleaners, or just air them out on the clothesline or in the dryer on "Cool Air." Launder curtains.

4. Wipe down all walls. Use a weak solution of mild ammonia and water to remove visible dirt and invisible mold and pollens. Remove pictures and plaques from the walls as you wash them. Wear rubber gloves and be careful not to cut your hand on exposed nails. Wash baseboards, doors, door frames, and window frames. You may decide to paint if washing just doesn't liven the room.

5. Clean the floors. Shampoo carpeting. Wash throw rugs. Strip and re-wax wood or linoleum floors if needed.

6. Redecorate dull rooms as your budget allows. Perhaps it's time to recover the sofa or replace that worn rug. Maybe you want to make a new tablecloth and curtains out of a couple of sheets you found on sale. If you enjoy crafts, make a new flower arrangement or wall hanging. Crochet a pretty afghan for that bare rocker sitting in the corner. Not all redecorating has to be expensive, and small touches can really brighten a room.

7. Re-arrange what you already have. It's amazing how moving the furniture or grouping some pictures on the wall can achieve dramatic results. Try to group similar objects in one place, such as all your figurines or your collection of pill boxes. Place furniture in a more practical, use-oriented arrangement, such as making an entertainment area near the stereo and TV. Design a quiet area for reading or table games. This is your chance to use your dormant creativity. You can make a room look like new without spending a cent.

8. *Eliminate clutter.* Clutter is your enemy! Simplicity is your friend! They cannot cohabit. Search out the clutter in your home and eliminate it. Many people live under the false impression that beauty comes from the over-accumulation of things. We need to take the oriental attitude that beauty comes from a proper balance between occupied and empty space. I once read that "simplicity, when taken to the extreme, becomes elegance." Allow your home to have the elegance of graceful, peaceful spaces.

Take a lesson from the decorators of display homes. By using only the absolute minimum of items needed to make each room functional and attractive, they create beauty and spaciousness. Begin by seeing how much you can eliminate from each room in your house. (Yes, you can store it in the basement until you're sure this is what you want to do!)

Most homes have too many pieces of furniture crowding the floors, too many pictures and plaques hanging on the walls, and too many knick-knacks crammed onto tabletops and shelves. Even our garages become so stuffed that we can no longer park our cars in them. Society's answer is to have bigger closets, more shelves and cabinets, and larger homes. As one writer put it, "It is time to awaken to the fact that conformity to a sick society is to be sick."[1] The more sane approach is to remove as many of our non-essentials as possible and allow each room to breathe. Our goal should be to see how little, rather than how much, we can be happy with.

The big bonus of eliminating clutter is that the less you have in each room, the easier its upkeep becomes. Living by the "Less is more" motto conserves money, time, and energy. As every backpacker knows, the lighter the load, the more enjoyable the trip. Many Christians have shirked their obligation to be the salt of the earth and the light of the world because they're too busy with the maintenance of their possessions. We become indistinguishable from the world in our collecting and comparing.

The pursuit of more things ultimately drives us from our homemaking careers. We spend time earning the money to buy our possessions, then we spend time shopping for them, then we must invest precious hours in cleaning, repairing, and maintaining them. Remember that anything you own also, in turn, owns you. The less our possessions encumber us, the more we can allow God to own us. Can we have a better motivation to eliminate clutter?

9. Reorganize everything that you decide to keep. Store things where you'll use them. Group similar items together. Bring order to your possessions as you deep clean each room in your home. Our God is a God of order. Order reflects His presence in our homes and in our lives. And it makes things a whole lot easier to find.

Suggestions for the Bathroom

1. Install a separate towel bar for each member of the family, assigning one to each person. Instruct them to hang their wet towels there after bathing. There is no reason a bath towel can't be used more than once by the same person, saving you the equivalent of one mountain of laundry per week. A couple of times each week gather all the towels and throw them into the wash during your thirty-minute touch-up time. After they're dry, rehang them on their towel bars. This eliminates time wasted on folding and putting them away.

2. Purchase a small plastic crate for each family member to store his or her personal toiletries under the sink or on

a shelf. If space is a problem, make a rule that one basket per person is the limit.

3. Eliminate a lot of bathroom quarrels by purchasing a tube of toothpaste for each family member to keep in his or her basket. Then anyone can squeeze in the middle or leave the cap off without upsetting those who prefer to do it differently.

4. Keep your own cosmetics and skin care products to a minimum to save space and money. Nobody needs 47 different shades of lipstick, eye shadow, and nail polish! Display them in a pretty basket or on a cosmetics tray. Keep it neat and clean. Few things are less attractive than a drippy, oozing, make-up mess.

5. Store toweling neatly folded under the vanity or on wicker shelving where it can double as part of your room decor. Throw those ugly, shredding towels into the rag box and use your pretty ones. Don't be like a certain grandmother who stored away her prettiest linens in a chest to pass on to future generations. When she passed away her children couldn't bear to use the things that she had denied herself, so they gave them all away.

6. Give each family member a personal clothes hamper for his or her room. A large plastic wastebasket or diaper pail works well. Just remember that if it has a lid on it, they won't use it. Tell them to throw their clothes in their own hamper instead of in the bathroom.

7. Keep bathroom decorations to a minimum to avoid clutter and keep cleaning simple. If it isn't a functional item, think twice before putting it there.

8. Keep everything used in the bathroom in the bathroom. Keep everything else out of the bathroom, including scuba gear, hamsters, and magazines.

9. Use lemon-oil furniture polish to remove soap scum from glass shower doors. My friend Geri taught her family to use a squeegee on the doors after each shower. Your husband might not go for this, but the kids will love it.

10. Keep a can of cleanser next to the tub and instruct family members to wash out their own rings after each bath.

Suggested Bathroom Rules

1. Whoever uses the last of anything (soap, toothpaste, etc.) is responsible for writing it down on Mom's shopping list. No one can complain if Mom doesn't buy something that isn't written down.

2. Anyone leaving a mess in the bathroom gets to clean the whole bathroom. Your kids won't forget this rule after the first infraction.

3. Whoever uses the last arm's length of toilet paper must put up the new roll. This rule avoids having your kids leave just one square.

Suggestions for the Master Bedroom

1. Clean out and rearrange your closets and drawers. (See Chapter 6.)

2. Launder all sheets, blankets, and mattress pads. Air out pillows. If pillow covers are wearing, purchase new zippered pillow covers.

3. If you don't have a ceiling fan, you can put a small, clip-on fan on your headboard. You can also purchase tiny, clip-on lights for late-night reading without disturbing your spouse.

4. Explore new ways to make your bedroom a cozy, attractive private place for you and your husband. Put scented oil rings on the lamps. Install a dimmer switch on the overhead light. Put a tape player in the room with an assortment of mood music. Use your imagination!

5. Consider rearranging the furniture for a new look. After we installed new bedroom carpeting last year, my husband asked, "Why don't we try putting the bed on a different wall?" My first response was negative, but we tried it and

he was right. That simple change made the room look twice as attractive as it did before.

6. Try making a tempting reading corner with a comfortable chair, a warm afghan, and a lamp. Put a basket of magazines next to the chair.

7. Make a place for your husband to put his personal things when he changes clothes after work. He will be less likely to throw items on the bed or the floor if he has a convenient place to put them.

8. Be sure you have a lock on your door to insure privacy. Teach your children to knock when your door is closed—and do the same for them.

Suggestions for the Children's Bedrooms

1. Wash all bedding and turn the mattress.

2. Arrange closet rods and shelves so that children can reach them to put away their own things.

3. Use inexpensive shelving and plastic crates to organize toys, books, and puzzles.

4. If the room is too crowded to clean well, why not create a playroom in an unused room of the house or in the basement? If you can do this, put all toys in the playroom, leaving only stuffed animals and books in the bedroom.

5. Give each child his own clothes hamper and teach him how to use it daily.

6. Make sure school-aged children have a well-lit study desk or table with pencils, paper, etc. This encourages better study habits.

7. Post a calendar and personal household duties schedule for each child in his or her own room. Encourage self-reliance by teaching the child to refer to this often.

Special Projects for Family Rooms

1. Consider creating use-oriented spaces. Make a quiet corner for table games or reading. Make an entertainment area

around the stereo and television. Make a sewing or crafts corner.

2. Move furniture if traffic patterns are wearing paths in the carpeting.

3. If you don't use your formal living room except for baby showers and funerals, consider converting it to some other use. Make it the children's playroom. Make it your personal office or craft room. Make it an upstairs laundry room. Or let your husband put a pool table in it. It's too expensive to heat and air-condition an unused room.

Special Projects for the Dining Room

1. Remove everything from the china cabinet and clean it well. Wash or polish everything that you took out. Before putting everything back into the china cabinet, evaluate it. Do you ever use that silver cranberry dish? Do you really want to polish it again next year? Wouldn't it make a nice gift for your niece in Pittsburgh? Don't keep an item just because someone else gave it to you. It was probably once a white elephant in their china cabinet.

2. Evaluate your table linens. Do you have too many? Do you have enough? If you can sew a straight line, you can make matching tablecloths and napkins from fabrics or sheets. See if you have a tablecloth for your table with all the leaves in it, with only one leaf in it, and with no leaves. You'll use that table more often if you do. Make your own napkin rings out of ribbons, lace, or fabric. Get creative!

3. See if you can use any of those rarely utilized serving pieces as decorations for your home. A platter with a letter opener on it makes a perfect place to put each day's mail. A bowl makes a good centerpiece when filled with silk flowers. A pretty glass can hold cut flowers from the garden. Use what you have rather than letting it gather dust in a dark cabinet. With just a little thought, you can use many household objects as decorative items.

4. As you work, make a list of anything you would like to add to your dining room. Write it down in your personal notebook under "Want List" (see Chapter 7) for the next time someone asks what you would like for Christmas or your birthday. Otherwise you'll never remember it, and you may receive another cranberry dish instead.

Special Projects for the Kitchen

1. Clean out drawers, cabinets, and pantry. Install new shelf paper if needed. If your shelving is too crowded, see what you can discard. How many pots and pans can you put on your stove at one time? How many plastic butter tubs can one person use? Are you expecting Tupperware to go bankrupt soon? Do you really want to wash and rearrange this item again next year? If not, get rid of it or put it in the basement and see if you ever miss it.

2. Group similar items together for easy access. Put all glass bottles and jars on the same shelf. Organize all canned goods, all baking supplies, and all paper products on another. Have a box for the metal gadgets and another box for the plastic ones in your small utilities drawer. Then you have half as much to root through to find something.

3. Clean out your spices, throwing out any over a year old. When you buy new spices, label their date of purchase with a piece of masking tape. A good place for storing spices is on little lazy Susans in the small cabinet space that most kitchens have over the stove. Or put them in a drawer, name side up.

4. Clean the oven and oven racks.

5. Clean the refrigerator and freezer.

6. Reorganize your cookbooks and get rid of that pile of magazine recipes that you've been meaning to use for the past ten years.

7. Make sure you have a two- to four-week's supply of food on hand in case the truckers strike or a natural disaster

occurs. Have you ever noticed the panic at the grocery store over something as small as a forecasted snow storm? Keeping a decent supply of food on hand is a prudent precaution.

Special Projects for the Basement

1. Clean walls, floors, and windows. Paint walls and floors with a light, water-sealing paint.

2. Get everything off the floors and onto wall shelving.

3. Have your furnace and air-conditioner cleaned and serviced for safety and longer life. Buy a year's supply of furnace filters. (Make a note of their size in your purse notebook. See Chapter 7.)

4. Spray for insects. Call the termite man and ask for a free inspection. They usually charge only if you're moving.

5. Get rid of everything you don't need and don't want to clean and rearrange again next year. This includes dried-up paint cans, rusty bicycles, and Tinker Toys if your children are now in college.

Special Projects for the Garage

1. Drag everything out of the garage. Sweep the floor, cleaning up grease and oil spots.

2. Get rid of everything you don't need, and don't put it back there!

3. Get everything possible off the floor. Use one shelf for auto-care products, one shelf for garden chemicals, and one shelf for barbecue supplies. Put garden tools, shovels, etc. on the wall. Hardware stores now carry many neat organizers for garages.

4. If you have a garage window, make sure it's clean and the curtain is in good repair. The appearance of your garage from the outside is as important as the rest of your house.

5. If you have a front-entry garage door, train the family to keep the garage door closed. Do you have a place where

you could install a side access door? The inside of a garage is rarely a pretty sight.

These are all just suggestions to help you get started on those deep-cleaning, reorganizing Special Projects. Use them all, or none at all. You'll surely think of many new ideas as you go along. Don't try to do it all the first time around; just do what you can find the time for. You won't do it at all if you dread it, so make it as pleasant as possible. Just remember that your primary goal is to be happy with that room at the end of the month.

Action Assignments

1. Choose a weekly time for your Special Projects, whether it be one morning a week or during your weekly cleaning time.

2. Make a monthly list of goals for your Special Projects.

3. Itemize the things you plan to accomplish this month during your Special Projects time, and check them off as you accomplish them.

4

Getting It Together

"Oh, for heaven's sake! Nothing is going right today," Margie complains for the tenth time. And, indeed, nothing is going right for Margie.

She is rooting through her drawers and cabinets for a measuring tape so she can figure out what size curtains she needs for her living room window. She's already upset because she bought curtains last week only to discover that she ordered the wrong size. Today she has to return them. At first she couldn't find her sales receipt, and now she can't find the tape measure. Little does Margie know that when she gets to the store to reorder the right sized curtains, she'll find that they don't come in the same shade of blue that she ordered the first time. Then she won't know which of the other shades of blue are right. Is this one too dark? Does that one have too much green in it?

Yes, Margie is having a bad day, and it's only going to get worse. The saddest thing about it is that Margie could have avoided all these hassles if only she knew the tips that you're going to learn from reading this chapter. After "getting it together" by making little organization areas in your home, you will never again suffer the needless frustrations that are overwhelming Margie today. You will have, as your mother always said, "a place for everything, and everything in its place." You may even have it a whole lot more "together" than your mother ever did. The whole purpose of this is not only to avoid needless irritations, but also to save time. Every minute you save by being organized is another minute you can spend on doing things you like to do. That makes the time you invest in this chapter time well spent.

Your Receipt Box

How many times have you thrown away or misplaced a receipt, only to regret it later? You tried on that pretty new sweater and it looked fine. How could you know that three weeks later the seams would start to unravel? You thought you had a great bargain on that pair of shoes until they developed a squeak with every step. Or you bought a dress for your niece's birthday only to learn that it was the wrong size and needed to be exchanged.

I'm sure you can think of dozens of instances when it would have saved you time and money if only you could find that elusive sales receipt. Many stores will give you a cash reimbursement for any sale item if you can prove that you paid full price for it in the past week or two. Some stores will allow you to return a purchase months later if you haven't used it and can prove you bought it there. But it's such a bother to keep those little slips of paper around, and you can never remember where you placed them even if you didn't throw them away. The only sane answer is to make yourself a receipt box.

You can make a receipt box out of an old cardboard shoe box or out of a pretty metal cookie tin. Mine is a small hinged plastic chest that I bought at a garage sale for ten cents. Just be sure to put the box in one spot and leave it there all the time. The best spot is probably in or near your desk. (See Chapter 5.)

Once you have your receipt box, you must adhere to only one rule: *Save every receipt*. Never throw one away. Never leave one in the paper grocery bag. Never fall prey to the temptation that "I surely won't need this one," because that's the very one you will need. Just get in the habit of throwing every receipt in your receipt box as soon as you get home. If the receipt is not from a computerized register that automatically itemizes your purchase, note that on the receipt before dropping it into the box.

At the end of each month put all your receipts in an envelope and mark it with the month and year. At the end of the year, place all your monthly envelopes into one large manilla envelope and date it with the year. Place it in your filing cabinet in the "Taxes and Finances" section. (See Chapter 5.) Your receipts can serve as valuable tax records. Best of all, your receipts can prove invaluable in budgeting for the next year. You'll know exactly where all the money went and which months had the heaviest expenses last year.

Your receipt box helps you save money now on any necessary returns or exchanges, and it also helps you to budget more wisely for future purchases. Best of all, it doesn't cost you a cent. Now that's what I call a bargain!

Your Toolbox

If you don't already have your own personal toolbox, I urge you to get one. No woman should have to root through her husband's stuff for any reason. First, you probably will waste time looking for whatever you need. Second, every time your husband can't find something, he will automatically assume that you were the one who misplaced it. It's wonderful to be able to say, "I never go near your tools, honey. I've got my own."

You don't have to rush out and buy a fancy red steel toolbox, although that can be an advantage if you want to put a lock on it. (This is not a bad idea—my husband and sons have already misplaced two whole sets of my tools.) You can simply make a toolbox out of a peck basket from the vegetable man, or out of a shoe box. I covered my peck basket with leftover wallpaper. You might want to glue lace and buttons on yours. There's no rule that says a woman's tool box can't be pretty!

Here are some suggested items to put in your toolbox:

- a small claw hammer
- an assortment of regular and Phillips head screwdrivers
- a box of small nails and screws
- a measuring tape
- a small pad and pencil
- a packet of felt stick-on pads to protect tables from being scratched by figurines, etc.
- some white all-purpose glue and some super glue

Put anything in your toolbox that you may need for the maintenance projects that you do around the house. Be sure to do what I've finally learned to do—mark your tools with colored tape or red fingernail polish so that you can identify them when they get borrowed by other people.

Your Errand Bag

Have you ever driven to the library and realized that you forgot to bring the books you wanted to return? Ever get to the cleaners only to find that you forgot to bring the dirty clothes? How many times have you walked into the grocery store without your shopping list and coupons?

These and many other frustrations can be eliminated by making yourself an errand bag. Mine is just a large plastic beach tote. You could just as easily use a large shopping sack or a box with handles. The important thing is to have an easily-carried container where you can place whatever needs to go on your next round of errands.

Keep your errand bag in the bottom of the coat closet or right next to the door so you don't forget it when you leave. In it place anything that needs to go somewhere else. A birthday present you need to take to a friend. The kid's video that needs to be returned to the store. Your husband's shoes that need to be repaired. The package that needs to go to the post office.

Your errand bag not only saves time by eliminating last-minute searches through the house, but it also saves the time, gasoline, and frustration spent on extra trips. An added bonus is that your errand bag eliminates the clutter of all those little "orphans" stranded in your house that have no place where they belong. Now they have an out-of-the-way place to stay until they leave. Best of all, your life is a little bit simpler.

Your Decorating Kit

Even though you may have no intention of redecorating your home, it's wise to keep a decorating kit in your car. You never know when you might come across a terrific sale on tablecloths, the prettiest little pillow, or a gorgeous picture that might be just the thing for your bedroom. You just never know when you'll need to decide whether something will look right in a particular place in your home. And you never want to buy the wrong thing. How can you know if that item is the right shade of green, or if it will clash with the pattern in your wallpaper? I can't think of a better way than by having your own decorating kit on hand.

A decorating kit is simply a large folder or envelope filled with little pieces and snippets of things from your home. In it place paint chips or scraps of wallpaper from the rooms in your house. Put a little silk flower from the arrangement on your coffee table. Include a sample of your carpeting.

(You can cut a sliver from the edge of a covered floor vent.) Save a snip of fabric from your reupholstered sofa. Add a piece of linoleum from the new kitchen floor. Fill your kit with anything and everything that you might ever need to help match or coordinate any future purchases you make for your home. It's even better if you throw in a few color snapshots of the rooms in your house.

In your decorating kit you can also place a small notebook filled with information about sizes of tables, windows, beds, or anything else that would help you get the right-sized item. Do you know what size tablecloth you need for your dining room or kitchen table? With one leaf, or two? When making up your decorating kit, take note of these things and you'll have the information forever.

Now keep that folder in your trunk or under a car seat and forget it—until the next time you just can't decide whether to buy the lavender candy dish or the blue one. The answer is as close as your decorating kit.

Your Check-Out Book

Are you a book lover? Do you collect books? Do you love to lend those books to friends? Do you wish to ever have them back again? If so, you should make yourself a check-out book.

Use a small blank-page book or little spiral notebook to keep track of all those favorite books, magazines, and tapes that you loan to friends. We all know that every friend intends to return those things soon, but too many of them get misplaced and forgotten. I've learned that the only way I remember who borrowed what is to keep track of it in my check-out book. There I write the name of the person, the item lent, and the date. Months later when I'm wondering where in the world my favorite cookbook has gone, I look in my check-out book and see that I lent it to Mary Lou. I simply give her a call and ask, "Are you finished with that cookbook I lent you on April 17?" "Oh, did I forget to return that to you?" she asks. "I'll bring it over right away."

Keep your check-out book and a pen right in your bookshelf. When someone borrows a book, write it down immediately or you'll forget. When they return the book, cross it off. Be sure to write your name and phone number in the front cover of all your books, too. It helps the borrower to remember where it came from so she can return it without being asked.

Don't wait too long before asking a friend to return a book. Once I asked for a book over a year after I lent it only to be told, "I'm sure I gave that back to you a long time ago." Three months is plenty of time for someone to borrow a book. If they haven't read it by then, they never will.

"Never a borrower or a lender be," unless you have a check-out book. Then your books will always return, like little lost sheep, wagging their bookmarks behind them.

Your First Aid Center

If your medications are cluttering and overflowing the medicine cabinet, drawers, and counter tops, you can quickly make a first aid center. Simply purchase several rectangular plastic baskets and place a masking-tape label on the handles.

Mark one label "Colds/Allergies." In that basket place all your over-the-counter and prescription remedies for coughs, colds, and sniffles. This includes antihistamines, cough syrups and lozenges, and nasal sprays.

Mark another basket "Stomach." In that basket place any medications for stomach or intestinal upsets, such as antacids, kaopectate, and laxatives.

Label another basket "Pain." This one is for any pain relievers such as aspirin, acetaminophens, ibuprofen tablets, ear drops, sore muscle rubs, and prescription pain relievers.

Then make a basket marked "Skin Care" for adhesive bandages, gauze and tape, ace wraps, and medications for the skin. These can include aloe gel for burns, mercurochrome (it doesn't burn like iodine), cortisone cream, suntan lotion, and anything else you may have for wounds or rashes.

In your last basket place your thermometer, ice bag, and heating pad. This is a good place to put booklets with first aid instructions. Be sure you have syrup of ipecac and instructions for how and when to treat poisoning, along with your local poison control phone number. Include a card with CPR (cardio-pulmonary resuscitation) instructions, and review them periodically. Sign up your family for a CPR and first aid class. Your teenagers will get more babysitting jobs if they let parents know that they've been trained in CPR and the Heimlich maneuver.

Where should you put your first aid baskets? They must be in a safe location away from children—yours and other's. You never know when you'll have an unexpected, or even uninvited, visitor. We once had a little neighbor boy who was an expert at sneaking into houses unannounced and consuming anything in sight, including my neighbor's birth control pills and my make-up! The best place I can think of for keeping your first aid center is on the very top shelf of your linen closet. Be sure to install a lock on the door.

Once a year, while doing your "spring cleaning," be sure to go through all your first aid supplies and throw out any expired medications. Make a list of anything you need to restock. Write the purchase date of any medications on the label before putting them away. Then you'll be comfortable knowing that you are prepared for any emergency.

Your Cleaning Center

Let me send you on an impromptu scavenger hunt. Can you quickly find the following items?

1. Dustpan and brush
2. Bucket and sponge

3. Clean dustcloth
4. Floor wax
5. Silver polish
6. New vacuum sweeper bags
7. Squeegee and window cleaning solution

Time's up—did you find them all? Were they located in one convenient place or did you have to do a lot of searching? Did you find the bucket in the garage, the silver polish in the back of the china cabinet, and all the other cleaning supplies scattered in cabinets and drawers throughout the house?

If you had any trouble locating these items, the simple solution is to make yourself a cleaning center. Your cleaning center is one specific place where you store all your cleaning tools and chemicals. The purpose for having it is to save time and effort—and to avoid scavenger hunts. It can be located wherever you want to put it.

One good spot for establishing your cleaning center is in a laundry room closet, if you're fortunate enough to have one. If not, how about making a special place in a corner of the garage, or in the pantry, or some unused closet in the house? If none of those places are available to you, there is another possibility—the linen closet. Almost every house or apartment has a linen closet. Most linen closets just become cluttered repositories of old sheets and pillowcases plus an odd assortment of other equally unused items.

If you have a washer and dryer at home, how many sets of sheets do you really need for each bed? My guess is only two—one set on the bed, which you wash and put right back on each week, and an old set for a spare. Keeping more than two sets of sheets per bed is an extravagance if you don't have space for a cleaning center. Donate your extra sheets— and anything else you don't use—to charity or put them in a garage sale. Then store your one extra set of sheets plus any extra blankets in a drawer, a chest, or in underbed cardboard storage boxes. Or you can lay them flat between the mattresses. Towels and washcloths should be kept in the bathroom. Now you have space in which to make your cleaning center!

To convert the linen closet to a cleaning center, simply remove all but the top two or three shelves, leaving enough room below them to accommodate your vacuum cleaner and broom. Install hooks around the sides and back wall for hanging your sweeper attachments, mops, and brooms. Save the top shelf for your first aid center if needed. Use the other shelves for storing your cans and bottles of cleaning chemicals. If there is room next to your vacuum sweeper, purchase a small utility cart with shelves for storing items such as your clean rags, sweeper bags, sponges, squeegee, etc. Otherwise store them in a bag hung on a wall hook. If room permits, you may also want to have a basket for storing light bulbs and a small one for storing unused extra batteries. (Can you ever find them when you need them?) This is also the perfect place for storing your toolbox.

As a very important safety precaution, install a lock on the door of your cleaning center to prevent accidental poisoning of a child. Even if your kids are grown, you'll feel better when guests bring children over to visit if you know that your cleaning chemicals are behind a locked door. Once you've created your cleaning center, you'll wonder how you ever did without it.

Your Family Message Center

The most likely place for your family message center is probably in your kitchen—everyone shows up there sooner or later during the day. Install a bulletin board with a pad and pencil near the telephone. Post a family activities calendar with plenty of room to write down everyone's appointments. Have the children write in their afterschool activities and sports practices. Enter important dates from their school calendar onto the family calendar as well.

Instruct all family members in the correct manner of answering the telephone. "Smith residence, Sandy speaking. No, she isn't available. May I take a message?" Then instruct them to always *write* down the message—otherwise it will be forgotten—and put the note on the bulletin board.

Be sure to place a pad and pencil next to every telephone in the house to insure that messages will be taken. If your family members have to walk to the kitchen to write it down, they may get distracted.

The family message center is also the place to put inter-family memos such as "I need the car Friday night" or "Can someone drive me to Francie's house Sunday at 2:00 p.m.?"

Note: Don't allow very young children to answer the telephone. Have you ever tried to get a talkative toddler off the line? "Can you *please* call your mother to the phone, Sweetie?" This can be very annoying to the caller, but worse yet, it can be a dangerous situation for a child not mature enough to understand how to handle calls from strangers.

Your Perpetual Telephone Book

If there's anything I hate to do, it's re-writing a new family telephone/address book. But every couple of years it needs to be done. People change addresses and phone numbers; family friends come and go; and you change the businesses that you patronize. Before long your book is full of scratched-out, scribbled-in changes, and it needs to be totally re-done. But not if you have a perpetual telephone/address book.

To make one, purchase a standard three-ring notebook with a small sized ring binder inside. One with pockets on the inside covers is best. Also buy a package of 26 tabbed dividers marked with each letter of the alphabet. Purchase some "Post-it" stick-on notepads.

Here's how to assemble a new perpetual telephone/address book. Use a separate "Post-it" sheet to write each person's name, address, and phone number. Then stick it on the appropriate page of the alphabet. Put all information for friends and relatives on the right-hand page, and information for stores, doctors, etc. on the left-hand page (the backside of the preceding divider.) If you have a lot of numbers to keep, you can overlap the stick-on notepapers—just be sure to write the name at the bottom of the paper rather than at the top. If you still need more room, just buy two sets of alphabet divider pages—one for family and friends and the other for business numbers—keeping both sets in the same notebook. In the front of your book be sure to include a page for all emergency phone numbers: police, fire department, poison control center, nearest hospital, ambulance, and others.

You can punch holes in your church directory and put that inside, too. Inside the front cover pocket keep menus from your favorite restaurants that deliver—the best information in the book!

Once you have made your new telephone book, you rejoice knowing that you'll never have to re-do the whole thing again. Whenever an address or phone number changes, all you have to do is pull out the old one and write up a new one to replace it. It will be easy to keep your family telephone book constantly up-to-date.

The Babysitter's Book

Purchase a spiral notebook to use exclusively for babysitter information. On the inside cover make a list of all important phone numbers: the poison control center, ambulance, police, fire department, pediatrician, and nearby relatives or next-door neighbors.

Below that make a checklist of things to show a new babysitter. Go over that list with her the first time she comes to your home. Show her where you keep your first aid center, where telephones are located, how to operate the door, locks, and light switches in your home, etc.

Then use the lined pages in your notebook to write specific instructions for each babysitter visit, which you can tear out after coming home. Write the phone number where you can be reached, the time you expect to be home, and who you prefer her to call if she can't reach you. Write down what snacks you allow the children to have, what TV shows they may watch, and what time the sitter should put them in bed. If they're taking medication, write down instructions for that as well. Note anything she needs to know such as, "The baby won't go to sleep unless she has her pink blanket and teddy bear." Your children and your sitter will appreciate the information. And you won't be worrying about them while you're supposed to be having a nice time away from home.

Keys, Please!

I hate to ask such an embarrassing question, but have you ever locked yourself out of the car? Wasn't it traumatic— and inconvenient? Didn't it make you feel foolish? These are very good reasons for making some extra sets of keys and putting them in some important places.

First, make sure that every family member old enough to use them has a house key and a set of car keys. Then make sure you have an extra set of each in a hidden place inside your house just in case someone loses a set. (Mine hang on a nail inside the coat closet.) Make an extra set of keys to give to a trusted neighbor if they are needed in an emergency, such as when you are out of town.

Then get an extra house key to keep in a hidden place outside your house in case you or the children are locked out. (Your trusted neighbor won't always be home.) Just wrap the key in a plastic bag and find a good spot that a burglar wouldn't consider. (No, not under the doormat or flowerpot.) How about behind a loose brick, under a particular rock, or under the back deck? Put your heads together, come up with the best spot, and make sure everyone knows where it is. If someone uses the key, be sure it gets replaced.

Finally, get two extra sets of car keys for each car. Keep one set in your purse. Most women don't lock their keys and their purse inside the car at the same time. Keep the second set hidden in a magnetic holder somewhere on the outside of your car. I believe that getting locked out of the car—especially at night—is a greater risk than having a thief find the car key and steal the car. Besides, a car thief doesn't usually waste time looking for a key; he just breaks in.

This may seem like a lot of extra key making, but this small investment will avoid the trauma and inconvenience of having a family member locked out of the house or car, especially in the cold or at night.

Shortly after I hid an extra set of keys on the outside of the family car, my husband locked his keys in the car when we went to church. He didn't realize his mistake until after the service. Being a basically wicked person, I let him stew for a minute before telling him where to find the extra key. But when he found that key, I got one big kiss. Talk about a lot of satisfaction for just a little effort!

These are a few sure-fire, family-tested suggestions for organizing your home and your life. Once done, you will be a happier, more organized, and "together" homemaker.

Action Assignments

1. Work on implementing all systems that you wish to use, but do them one at a time, completing one before beginning the next one.

2. Before beginning each project, make a shopping list of any items needed and have everything on hand.

3. Include the family by explaining the benefits of the new system and instructing them in its use.

5
Your Control Center

If you've ever watched a rocket launch, you've seen the control center from which all the activity of the event is conducted. Men and women sit behind rows of desks monitoring, directing, and correcting to make sure all goes according to plan. What's the result of their efforts? Everyone claps and cheers as a shining missile pierces the sky and disappears into outer space.

As the manager of a busy home and active family, you need a control center, too. You need a place where you can formulate and execute goals and projects for yourself and for your family. You need a central place in your home from which all production emanates. You need a control center so that you, too, can achieve your goals—keeping your home from careening out of control.

Your control center is, of course, your desk. More than just a desk, it is your "office." Whether it's a whole room or just a little nook in the corner of a room, your office is the place where you write letters, pay bills, plan, and organize. If you've never had an office of your own, this chapter can help to transform your life. If you already have one, this chapter can help you make it even better.

Finding a Place

The first step toward making an effective office is to decide upon its location in your home. When I decided that we needed an office and I couldn't find a place for one, I decided to do something drastic. I took over our seldom-ever-used, formal living room and converted it into an office. You should have seen the look on my husband's face the day he noticed there wasn't a stick of furniture in our previously furnished living room!

"Where is our furniture?" he gasped.

"I sold it," I smiled with all the feminine charm I could muster.

"You what?" he cried incredulously.

"We never used it anyway, and I'm going to make the living room into a place that really gets used," I said, trying to sound convincing. I gave him a reassuring pat and said, "Trust me."

My husband was even more shocked the day he found a large, old, battered desk sitting in the middle of the empty room—and me scooping goopy furniture stripper from it!

"Don't worry, honey. It's gonna look great!" I smiled.

By this time I guess he figured I was a hopeless case. But for many years now my husband and I have gotten a lot of use from that formerly idle living room. My desk, which I rescued from the back of a used furniture warehouse and spent hours refinishing, is used daily. Next to it we now have a computer desk. We have a filing cabinet, two armchairs with a table between them, pretty floral wallpaper, and family pictures on the wall. This is more a "living room" now than it ever was before, filled with constant activity. Even Gretel, our Dachshund, has squatter's rights to one of the chairs where she can sit at the window and bark at passers-by.

Maybe you don't have anything resembling a good spot for an office, and you can't imagine where to devise one.

You may need to make your temporary office in a spare dresser drawer or in an underbed cardboard box, and hope for more space of your own in the future. Better to have a tiny office than no office at all. Don't despise the day of small beginnings!

But chances are you, too, could find an under-utilized spot in your home—a living room, dining room, sitting area, or just a corner in the bedroom or kitchen. If so, make it into a functional office and get some real use out of that space. Think creatively and you'll probably find a great place for that new "control center" of your own.

Furnishing Your Office

Once you've decided on a location, you need a desk. Perhaps you already have a desk in an obscure area of your home, doing little more than gathering dust. If so, it's time you think about using it more productively. Perhaps you have a built-in desk in your kitchen, as many modern homes do. If you don't have a desk, you don't need to run to the nearest furniture store. You could rummage through some garage sales and find a used desk that just needs a little sprucing up. Or you could visit some re-sale shops like I did. If you let it be known that you need a desk, you might find a relative who has one he no longer wants. You can also make a desk by laying a door over two file cabinets—it creates a large work space and lots of storage space, too. Even a card table covered with colorful adhesive paper can serve the purpose until you find a desk that's just right for you.

Along with your desk you'll need a chair. I used a dining room chair until I got a great rolling office chair for $10.00 at a garage sale. Today discount stores sell desk chairs at a fraction of what they used to cost. If you have a spare wooden chair, you could attach casters to the legs and make it into a rolling desk chair. Just make sure it's a comfortable height for you or it can cause backaches.

Then you need some neat stuff to put in that desk of yours. Along with all your favorite photos and desktop memorabilia, you need some serious desk supplies. You need a lamp that will not glare in your eyes. You need a deskpad to protect it from scratches and ink marks. You may want to install a spare telephone at your desk, and maybe a phone answering machine.

Then you need "In and Out" trays—these are crucial. You can buy expensive teakwood trays, but I find the inexpensive plastic stacking trays work just as well. Get four. The top tray is for "To Do" material that you have not yet processed. The second tray is for "Bills To Be Paid." The third tray is to "Hold" for further action later. And the fourth tray is "To Be Filed." These trays will do wonders for your paper management!

After you bring in the mail from the mailbox, don't lay it in your "To Do" tray. Find another place to put each day's mail until you and your family have sorted through it. You can purchase a mail holder designed just for that purpose, or you can use a pretty basket, tray, or dish. Place the mail holder wherever it's most convenient for you; perhaps on your desk, or maybe on an end table or the kitchen counter. Keep a letter opener and a wastebasket near your mail holder.

My husband loves to sort through the mail every evening after work, so I leave everything, even the junk mail, there for him to browse through. (He thinks his middle name is "Occupant.") After he looks through it, all the discards go right into the trash. Any reading material, like magazines or catalogs, I place on our night tables so we can browse through them at leisure in the evening. The only thing that goes into the "To Do" desk tray are papers that need further processing at deskwork time. That leaves the "To Do" tray free from the clutter of junk mail, unwanted envelopes, or reading material.

Here are other supplies you may want to acquire for your office:

- Calendar
- Pens, pencils, markers
- Scissors
- Transparent tape
- Stapler and staple pull
- Paper clips (colored ones are more fun!)
- Rubber bands
- Ruler
- Envelopes
- Cards and stationery
- Note pads
- Calculator
- Your receipt box and monthly envelopes (see Chapter 4)
- Your perpetual telephone book (see Chapter 4)
- A wastebasket (your greatest ally in the war against paper clutter!)

I keep my greeting cards in a separate box that has dividers marked for the type of card (birthday, thank you, or plain). This allows plenty of room for storage and protects them from damage.

Have you ever wondered what to do with personal cards and letters that you receive? Do you regret throwing them away, or do you stuff them into any available spot and worry about what to do with them later? If so, you may want to start storing them in a large zip-lock bag in your desk drawer. Buy the kind of bag that you can write on, then write the year on the outside of the bag. At the end of the year you can store it in your memorabilia box. (I keep a large cardboard box for each member of the family stored in the basement. That's where I store treasures that we don't want to throw away, such as special artwork, letters and cards, etc.)

If you have a typewriter, your new office is the perfect place to keep it accessible, rather than having to drag it out every time you want to use it. Keep a good supply of paper and correction tape on hand. This is also the perfect place for your computer. If you aren't "computerized" yet, you may want to consider it. In the future most families will consider a computer to be as indispensable as a television set. It's a great way for children to learn to operate the latest technology—not to mention play computer games! As they get older, they may want to use it to do their homework, too.

More and more adults, and especially homemakers, are learning that the home computer is a real time saver. You can learn to use the word processor for writing letters and club bulletins, or you can write a book! You can use the database to keep track of a myriad of information, such as your budget, your recipes, or your Christmas card list. If you're interested in learning more about computers for home use, consult your community college or evening adult education classes at the high school. I resisted learning this new technology at first, but now I'm so glad I did it. You will be, too!

Your Filing System

The next most indispensable item that belongs in your office is a file cabinet. No, you don't have to be a business office to need a file cabinet; you just need to be a busy family. Without my file cabinet I would never be able to find anything. It saves a lot of squabbles, too. No more irritated voices saying, "I didn't lose it—you were the last one who had it! How am I supposed to keep track of every little piece of paper?" Now that we have a functional filing system, I often wonder how we ever found anything before using the "stuff it wherever you can find an empty spot" system.

If you don't have a file cabinet, you don't necessarily need to buy an expensive metal drawer-style cabinet. Department stores and office supply centers now carry great sturdy cardboard boxes made for that purpose for only a couple of dollars. If you want to, you can cover one or more with attractive adhesive paper and use them as part of your decor. You can even stack a couple to use as an end table.

Before we get into the specifics of how to set up your filing system, it's important to keep one thing in mind. According to one estimate, eighty percent of papers filed are never looked at again! To avoid creating an ever-growing filing-system monster, it's imperative that you set aside a time each year to go through every piece of paper in your filing system. Thin out your file by discarding unneeded papers, and re-organize anything that got misfiled. The best time to do this is early in the year, before tax time. It could be your Special Project for the month to clean the office, desk, and files. (See Chapter 3.)

You'll also need to purchase a box of manilla folders. Then gather all your family papers and sort them into logical divisions. Rather than having a random assortment of alphabetically arranged file folders, divide them into major categories and sub-categories. I bought some colored posterboard paper and made tall dividers to mark major categories. (Just draw an outline of a regular file folder onto the posterboard, but add a couple of inches at the bottom so it will stand higher than the other folders.)

For instance, the first major category divider in our file cabinet is marked "Automobiles." Behind that are file folders for each of the sub-categories: a folder for "AAA" auto club information, then "Ford" for papers related to my car, then "Misc. Auto Info." for clippings regarding car care, and then a folder marked "Van" where we keep all papers related to my husband's car. Inside each of the folders for our cars we keep every piece of paper relevant to that car, including receipts from state inspections and repairs and maintenance, including oil changes. (I know a woman who used her records to win a court case against a car dealer who refused to honor her warranty. He said he didn't have to replace defective parts on her car because she hadn't changed the oil on schedule. But she had written proof that she did!)

Set up another major category for "Family Information" with folders for each family member's medical records, folders for medical and dental insurance papers, children's report cards, birth certificates, and other such personal papers. Behind "Household Information" you could have folders for keeping those dozens of little brochures and warranties that come with every appliance and gadget you own. Inside each brochure staple the warranty and a photocopy of your receipt, which also shows the date you purchased the item and its cost. You can also make a folder for keeping a copy of all information about your house, including a survey of your lot.

Make a major category for "Finances" where you keep folders regarding investments, loans, etc. In a folder marked "Credit Cards" keep photocopies of all credit cards and information on where to call if they are lost or stolen. Make a folder for "Taxes" where you throw any relevant information throughout the year, including W-2 forms, to make tax time a lot easier. Make a folder for "Misc. Financial Info." where you can keep magazine and newspaper clippings about budgeting and investments. Keep a copy of your will in a folder marked "Will," and let family members know where it is if they ever need it. Be sure to keep any irreplaceable important papers, such as original copies of your will, deeds, and car titles, in a safe deposit box. Make photocopies for your home filing system. Make a videotape or take photos of everything in your home to keep in your safe deposit box for insurance purposes.

It's nice to have one file drawer or box for important household information. Use another drawer to store your interests and hobbies. Under the major category of "Vacations" keep folders for each trip you've taken in the past so you can remember where you stayed and what you saw. Keep copies of maps, motel receipts, and sight-seeing brochures. It makes planning the next trip a lot easier. Collect brochures for planning new trips in another folder.

I keep a large category marked "Personal Interests." Behind that I have folders labeled with such unremarkable things as "Amish" (I love to collect articles and photos about the Amish), "Decorating," "Favorite Anecdotes" (I love funny stories), "Gardening," "Gift Records" (where I keep track of gifts I gave in the past to avoid duplication), "Politics" (for political information), "Prayers," and dozens more.

If you have a lot of information on one subject, you can make that a major category. If you enjoy collecting recipes, you could have the major category of "Recipes" with sub-category folders marked "Beef," "Casseroles," "Chicken," "Desserts," "Fish," etc. Then if that major category becomes too large, just give it a whole file drawer of its own. My "Quilting" file grew until it had to go into a separate filing box, which I now keep with my sewing supplies rather than in my office. Other major categories you might want to create could include "Bible Studies," "Crafts," or "Children's Interests."

Do you collect stacks of magazines that you can't bear to part with because you don't want to lose many of the photos and articles they contain? Has your stack become so large that you couldn't find something in there if you had to? Are you tempted to throw out the whole thing? Your filing system is a great place to resolve that problem. As you read your magazine, earmark the pages with information that you want to save. Then tear out just those pages and throw away the rest. (My husband says I don't know how to read a magazine without tearing it apart!) Then just drop those clippings (or photocopies of information from books) into the appropriate folder in your system, and you can retrieve them anytime you need them. With this system you never waste an idea—once you store it in your files, it's yours forever. Eventually you may become an information source for others. Or you just might write a book to share all the ideas you've gathered!

We just remodeled our kitchen, and I was glad to have many photos of kitchens in my "Decorating" folder to give me ideas. Whenever I get in the mood to crochet, I just pull out the folder that's stuffed with great patterns I've collected over the years. When reading magazines I also tear out any cartoons or articles that I think a friend or family member might enjoy. I lay them in the "To Do" tray on my desk until I sit down to write letters and enclose the clipping in the envelope. My sons at college often receive such little reminders that I'm always thinking of them.

Make a Goodie Bag

What do you do with catalogs and magazines that you no longer want? There are many ways to recycle such paper products other than sending them to the recycling center. Why not take them to a nearby hospital or leave them in the dentist's office the next time you visit?

One of my favorite things to do is to make little "goodie bags" for friends and nearby relatives. Whenever I have something I'd like to pass on to one of them, I just put their name on a paper sack or a pretty plastic bag (I save the nice ones for this purpose) and toss in the bag anything I come across that I think they would like. The last time I met my mother at the mall, I gave her a goodie bag that contained a jewelry catalog (she loves jewelry), a couple of family snap-shots (I get my film developed on free double-print days so I have something else to send in the mail and put in goodie bags), and a couple of pieces of dessert I had baked the day before.

The last time I saw my friend Dee I gave her a goodie bag that had a VCR tape of a television Bible teacher we both enjoy, a cartoon clipping, a bookmark, and a catalog. Right now I have a goodie bag waiting for the next time I see Fritzi. It contains several magazines that I didn't tear apart, a hand-me-down T-shirt for her son Nathan, and a snapshot of Fritzi sitting at my sewing machine the day she came over and we made vests together. (In fact, Fritzi's the one who got me in the habit of making goodie bags in the first place.)

This is a great habit to begin among friends—soon they'll get the idea and start giving goodie bags to you, too! It's a resourceful way to have something to give away at little or no expense. Keep your goodie bags in your errand bag so you'll have them with you the next time you're on the go. (See Chapter 4.)

As you can see, there are many creative ways to tame the paper tiger at your house. Your new control center not only helps you organize your papers—it helps you organize you. Your new office (no matter how small) is where you can do your daily planning and have your quiet time, as well as shuffle papers. It's important to have one regular day per week when you take the time to do deskwork. Perhaps one evening a week after you put the children to bed would be best for you. I enjoy doing my deskwork on idle Sunday afternoons. Find the day that best suits you, and mark it on your weekly schedule. (See Chapter 7.)

To keep your desk supplies from "walking off," it's wise to show your desk to your children (they're going to be curious!) and explain to them that they can't remove anything from your desk unless they receive permission from you. Then they'll probably want you to help them set up a desk of their own—which is the best idea yet!

Action Assignments

1. Select a location for your control center.
2. Equip your control center with a desk and a comfortable chair.
3. Make a shopping list and obtain any needed desk supplies.
4. Set up your new "In and Out" trays and filing system.
5. Find a permanent place to lay each day's mail until family members sort through it.
6. Keep reading material on a bedside table or in a large basket for later perusal.

7. Begin to make "goodie bags" for friends.
8. Show your children your new control center and explain the rule about not removing items from your desk.
9. Help your children set up a desk of their own where they can study and keep their own papers and supplies in order.

6

Classy Closets

"Honey, the boss asked me to take an important client and his wife out to dinner tonight, and I'd like you to go with me. Can you be ready in an hour and a half?"

When Ellen answered the telephone, that was the last thing she expected to hear. She stood there wondering how she would make the transformation from her present condition—she had been cleaning the house—to that of charming executive's wife, in only ninety minutes. She knew this was important to her husband, and she didn't want to disappoint him. The children were spending the night with a friend, so at least she wouldn't have to worry about finding a sitter.

"Well, I guess I can make it," Ellen replied before hanging up the phone. Then she jumped into the shower, blow-dried and fixed her hair, and put on her make-up in only forty-five minutes. "Great!" she said, "I've still got another forty-five minutes to get dressed, so I'll be ready in plenty of time."

That's when her troubles began. Ellen threw open her closet door only to face a confusing jumble of clothing and accessories. What on earth should she wear?

First, she pulled out a navy blue knit dress, put it on, and looked in the mirror. "Rats! I forgot about those deodorant stains under the arms. I meant to take this to the cleaners after I wore it the last time."

She pulled that off, messing her hair in the process, and tried on a black and white printed skirt and blouse. "Oh, no," Ellen sighed as she realized there were two buttons missing on the front of the blouse. She threw them on the floor next to the navy blue dress.

Next she donned a red and green plaid dress with a pleated skirt. When she tried to zip it up, Ellen remembered that she was about eight pounds lighter the last time she wore this dress. "Darn it!" she mumbled in exasperation as she rooted through her closet for something else.

Forty-five minutes and several unsuccessful outfits later, Ellen dashed out the door wearing that navy blue dress. "I'll just have to keep my arms down," she reminded herself. She was also wearing scuffed navy pumps and pantyhose with fingernail polish patching one end of a runner that she hoped wouldn't grow any bigger. She hadn't had time to put on a touch-up coat of nail polish, or to carefully select the proper jewelry and scarf.

Did Ellen have a good time at dinner? Of course not. Why? Because Ellen didn't feel good about herself that night. And Ellen didn't feel good about herself simply because her closet was a mess. If only she had taken a day to clean and organize her closet, Ellen would have enjoyed the beautiful restaurant, the delicious food, and the people she was dining with. But the only thing she could think about all evening was herself. Ellen learned a valuable lesson that night—one must think of herself ahead of time so that she can think of others later. The very next day Ellen organized her closet.

Make the Investment

Oprah Winfrey once said, "It changes your life to have your closet organized." She was right. A woman is not going to look any better than her closet does. The woman with the messy, disorganized closet is going to have that messy, disorganized look. But the woman who makes you look twice because she has that self-confident, classy appearance also has that secret ingredient—a classy closet.

Classy closets don't just happen, though. Like everything else worthwhile, they take an initial investment of time and effort. So before jumping headlong into that deep, dark closet, take a few minutes to do some planning.

First, set aside a day for that closet make-over. As a wise homemaker, you'll want to tackle this project on a day when you have a minimal amount of distractions. Send the children off to Grandma's for the day, or arrange for them to play at a friend's house. You may even want to strike a bargain with a neighbor. "If you keep the kids while I clean my closet, I'll return the favor for you."

Before you embark on that special "closet experience," make a shopping list. Take a look at what you have versus what you need, and buy your supplies in advance. You can, of course, pick up the phone and have someone come out and re-build your closet from scratch. If money is no object for you, this is the ideal way to do it. But for the rest of us who are accustomed to do-it-yourself projects, I suggest you consider purchasing whatever you need from the following list of closet spruce-up supplies:

- Light colored paint for walls and woodwork.
- Wallpaper. If you have a closet of your own, this is your chance to indulge yourself in that utterly feminine pink rosebud print that your husband can't stand.
- Shelf paper. Select something soft and pretty that you won't tire of.
- Specialty closet rods and shelving for making more space. A double rod is essential in at least part of your closet for hanging skirts, blouses, and slacks.

- An attractive light fixture. No bare, ugly bulbs will be allowed to mar the loveliness of your new closet.

- Good storage bags and boxes for out of season clothing. Don't allow last season's clothing to waste valuable space.

- Three cardboard boxes to use on closet cleaning day. Label them: "To Dry Clean," "To Repair or Alter," and "To Charity or Garage Sale."

- A plastic crate to keep in your closet. This is where you throw anything that needs to go to the dry cleaners or to be repaired. If you leave it on a hanger, you'll inevitably forget about it.

- Plenty of padded and plastic hangers. Good clip skirt hangers. Don't bother with gimmicky hangers where you hang several things on top of each other. You'll probably tire of bothering with them. Plan on throwing out all those old wire hangers.

- A couple of shoe racks. Get the simple metal floor-type or, if you have the wall space, the pocket-type is nice.

- A good quality belt hanger. Plastic ones usually break. The ring-type is a pain because you have to take off all the belts in front of the one you want, and then put all the others back. I have found a men's necktie rack to be the perfect belt hanger.

- Scarf hangers. Storing scarves in drawers always leaves them creased and flat. At a luggage shop I found some clip clothespin-type hangers for hanging washables when traveling. They have an over-the-rod hook and allow scarves to hang freely from the closet rod instead of laying folded. Or you may want to drape them on a mug rack.

- A full-length sheet glass mirror. You just can't be well-dressed without being able to see your whole self at once.

- A frilly sachet to give your closet a fresh, clean scent and make it as pleasurable for your nose as for your eyes.
- A good lint brush and a hook to hang it on.
- Hooks for hanging hats and accessories on unused wall-space.
- Organizers for storing purses and folded sweaters. Never put sweaters on hangers or they'll pull out of shape.
- A clothes hamper. A large diaper pail or plastic wastebasket works well.
- A shoe shine kit supplied with polish and clean rags. You can always tell how well-groomed a person is by looking at his or her shoes.
- A small pair of scissors for clipping tags and loose threads. Have you ever succumbed to the temptation to pull that little thread, and wished you hadn't? Hang the scissors on a hook.
- A small wastebasket to toss threads and tags into.
- Anything else you can think of that will make your closet, and therefore your life, a little nicer.

Once you've acquired your supplies and set aside a day all to yourself, you're ready to dig in and clean your way out. Before you start, be sure to make your bed and straighten your room. You want a cheerful atmosphere to work in, don't you? Put on your favorite closet-cleaning music, perhaps something inspiring and classical. Open a window and let the breeze freshen your room as you work. Pull back the curtains and let the sunlight pour in. After all, today is the day that you and your closet are making a fresh beginning. You may as well make it fun!

Getting Started

The first step is always the hardest, so just get it over with as quickly as possible. Yes—take everything out of your closet. Everything. The clothes. The shoes. The belts, scarves, sweaters, jackets, and all that weird stuff that you wonder how it ever got there in the first place. Pull it all out and throw it on the bed. When you finish, you should be staring at one naked closet. Shocking, isn't it? But don't worry, you are not just applying a Band-aid here; this is major surgery!

Next, replace that burned-out light bulb and shine up the fixture. Now you can see to wash down the walls and woodwork, shelves, and clothes rods. If you decided to paint or apply wallpaper, see how quickly you can get that done. Turn up the music and go at it with enthusiasm. "Whatever you do, do your work heartily, as for the Lord" (Colossians 3:23). When the walls are clean, put some fresh paper on the shelves. Finish up by washing or vacuuming the floor, and you'll have a pristine, clean closet looking back at you.

You have just completed Phase I: *emptying and cleaning*. It's time to fix a cup of tea, clear a spot on the bed, and relax a minute while admiring what you have accomplished. You haven't just emptied a closet—you have prepared a clean slate. From now on you are going to be very selective about what goes back in there. No more junk. Nothing questionable. Only classy clothes are going to be allowed into your classy closet.

If you share your closet with your husband, I suggest you replace his clothing first. (If he comes home before you finish, you don't want him to think you're moving him out!) As you probably know, living compatibly with your husband is much easier if each of you has your own closet. But if you must share, just choose the best side for yourself and make the most of it.

You might be able to think of a place where you can have a closet of your own. One woman I know moved her clothing into a spare bedroom. My husband and I shared a tiny walk-in closet until I discovered an alternative. I transformed a little-used sitting nook in our bedroom into a second closet. That closet is a lot more functional than that useless nook ever was.

Try On Everything

Now you are ready for Phase II: *trying on and sorting out.* Take time to try on each garment in front of your full-length mirror. (Yes, you'll have to put on your bra and panty-hose!) Carefully scrutinize each item. Before determining where that garment belongs, ask yourself the following questions:

1. Is it out of season? If so, be sure you clean and repair it before putting it in storage. Anything out of season is wasting your precious space.

2. Does it fit well? If the answer is no, it goes into the alteration box or the give-away box—not in your closet. If you have to lose "a couple of pounds" before it fits properly, store it with your out of season clothing. You don't want to look into your closet and see anything hanging there that you can't wear today.

3. Is it comfortable? If it isn't, you won't wear it. Get rid of it. It will surely be comfortable on someone else who could really get some use out of it.

4. Does it need cleaning, repair, or alteration? Put those items in the box so labeled.

5. Is this a flattering color for me? If you aren't sure, I encourage you to get yourself color analyzed. It's one of the best gifts a woman can give herself. If it isn't a color that's good for you, you'll never feel good about yourself when you wear it. Make it a gift to someone who would look better in it.

6. Can I mix and match this with other clothing? Try on new and different combinations to see how far you can make that item go. Different prints, stripes, and plaids can be attractively mixed if they are in the same colors. Completely different solid colors can be mixed if they are of the same intensity.

7. *Have I worn this in the past year?* If you haven't, why not? Perhaps your closet was so overcrowded that you forgot you had it. Or maybe you didn't realize it looked good with some other clothing you have. Or did it just need the hem shortened? If so, keep it. But if you didn't wear it because it's poorly constructed, doesn't look right on you, or you're just plain sick of it, get rid of it.

8. *Is this something I hate, but just feel too guilty to throw out?* If so, do it anyway. You won't save any money by letting it hang uselessly in your closet. Consider whatever you paid for it to be the price of experience. In the future you'll shop smarter. Besides, if it's given away it really isn't a waste.

Decide which garments are worthy of your classy closet, and then neatly hang them on an appropriate hanger. Put jackets on padded hangers, skirts on clip hangers, and fold slacks neatly on slacks hangers. Return all those nasty metal hangers to the dry cleaners for recycling. While you're at it, throw out all plastic dry cleaning bags and paper sacks—they are definitely not classy. You'll wear everything in your closet often, and you won't need to store clothing in bags.

Hang all your garments facing the same direction. Group blouses, slacks, etc., neatly together. See that all buttons are buttoned and zippers zipped. Of course, everything should be impeccably clean and pressed. Polish your shoes and purses and set them pertly in their proper places. Put belts and scarves where they belong. From now on, everything that goes into your closet is truly "ready to wear" in its best condition.

From now on, whenever you open that closet door you'll feel as pampered as if you had your very own boutique where everything was designed especially for you. Your most private, personal space has become your favorite place.

Every time you emerge from that closet, you're going to look as great as it does.

After seeing your closet transformed, you may very well want to tackle those dresser drawers, too. Why stop halfway? Group similar items together in the same drawer, and throw out all bags and boxes. Keep jewelry in a jewelry box, not scattered randomly in several drawers. If it won't all fit in your jewelry box, maybe it's time to give some of it away. Get rid of all your "holely" underwear and that ratty nightgown that turns off your husband. He surely won't mind when you get new ones. Make that dresser as neat and clean and classy as your clothes closet.

Attack your make-up stash in the bathroom. Do you really need 67 different shades of eye shadow? Or all those dried-up vials of fingernail polish? I know you have that shoebox full of samples and cosmetic rejects, too. Did you know that old make-up breeds bacteria? If you don't wear it, trash it. From now on set a limit to the space you'll allow for cosmetics, and don't fall prey to temptation in the drug store anymore. Just remind yourself of all those messy, drippy jars and bottles that you just threw out.

Your Want List

Now return to that closet for another good look at what you've accomplished. Once you've tried on every garment you own and determined its fate, you may be surprised at how bare your closet looks. "Good grief—I have a huge pile of cleaning, repairing, and give-aways, but very little in my closet!" you gasp. But that's good! It has been estimated that most women wear ten percent of their clothing ninety percent of the time. You've just weeded out some of those things that you never wore anyway to make room for the things that you really do enjoy and wear. Besides, your garments need space to breathe. "But this is too much breathing space!" you protest.

That's when you go into Phase III: *planning future acquisitions*. Once you've disposed of your give-aways and returned clean, repaired clothes to your closet, you're ready to make a list of needs and wants. Keep this list in your personal notebook that you carry in your purse. (See Chapter 7.) Sit down in front of your closet and thoughtfully plan what items you need to round out your wardrobe. Write the most important items at the top of your list.

Maybe you need a versatile, neutral-colored dress that you can dress up or down, depending on your accessories. Because you can get a lot of mileage out of this one piece of clothing, you should invest in quality merchandise. Perhaps you need a couple of fun blouses in bold colors to brighten a too-conservative repertoire. Write down anything and everything you would like to incorporate into that new classy closet of yours.

Then you must make a promise to yourself: in the future you must never buy anything—clothing, shoes, purse, or accessories—without first looking at your "want list." Seeing something that you really want will prevent you from making an impulse purchase of a "bargain" sale item. Remember, it isn't a bargain if you don't need it! And if it isn't on your list, you probably don't need it. When you find something you do need, be sure to consider the three "C's":

1. Comfort—Will you wear something that really isn't comfortable?

2. Color—Why settle for a color that is less than your best?

3. Coordination—Does it mix well with the rest of your wardrobe?

Your list will be invaluable the next time someone asks you what you would like to have for your birthday or Christmas. Never again will you stare blankly and say, "Oh, I really don't need anything." Instead, you'll say, "Well, there's a smashing pink and green silk scarf at my favorite dress shop!'' Why not allow them the pleasure of giving you something you'll really use?

The main advantage of your list, however, is to help you avoid future mistakes in your closet. It encourages you to purchase only those things you need. My friend Fritzi, a professional image consultant, teaches her students, "If you can wear something different every day for three or four weeks, you have too many clothes." She sees women who try to overcome their insecurity about how to dress well by over-buying. They try to substitute quantity for quality. Fritzi teaches them that it's much better to have a limited selection of quality clothing than to have a closet crammed full of misfits and make-dos.

You may want to take a class or read books that will help you avoid future clothing mistakes by determining the look that is right for you. Too often we try to look like someone we are not for the sake of wearing what is now popular. One author wrote, "Why not be oneself? That is the whole secret of a successful appearance. If one is a greyhound, why try to look like a Pekingese?"[1] If you are a full-time homemaker, why not look like a lovely homemaker instead of trying to look like a bank president or a rock star?

Confusion about who we are often causes us to follow every new fashion trend, regardless of what looks best on us. I once read that fashion says, "Me too," while style says, "Only me." Learn what style is really you based on your body proportion and lifestyle. Once you've found the right style and coloring for you, every piece of clothing you purchase will mix and match with a lot of other items in your closet. As a result you'll need less, so you can buy better quality.

Stretch Your Budget

Sometimes women feel too guilty to pay more for the quality we really want. The best way to determine whether a garment is worth the price is to calculate the cost per wearing. Divide the cost of the garment by the number of wearings to see what kind of buy you're getting. For example, a faddish dress that costs $60.00 and is worn only four times actually costs you $15.00 per wearing. But a well-made, classic styled dress that costs you $200.00 and you wear twice a month for the next couple of years costs you little more than $4.00 per wearing. So the "costlier" item was really the better buy.

Perhaps that's why the excellent wife in Proverbs 31 wore "fine linen and purple." That was as well-dressed as you could get in those days. But, far from being extravagant, she also did her own sewing. This is something that still works today for the woman who wants to dress well on a budget. I'm not a great seamstress, but I don't mind making a basic, simple skirt because I enjoy stretching my clothing budget. My friend Barb is an excellent seamstress who makes almost all the clothing for herself and for her children. She has developed her talent through taking sewing and tailoring classes, which are available to most of us who are willing to learn. She loves to economize while making things exactly the way she wants them.

Another way to economize is to purchase clothing that mixes and matches so that you need fewer items. I have a magazine article that shows how you can combine eight garments thirty different ways! Making each garment go a long way helps us resist the impulse to over-buy clothes. But clothes aren't the only thing we can over-purchase.

Eunice was a woman who owned hundreds of pairs of shoes. If anyone commented that her collection rivaled that of Imelda Marcos, Eunice would laugh and reply, "Well, at least I bought them all on sale." As a result, she had disorderly closets stacked full of shoes that she rarely wore. She couldn't even remember what shoes she owned, let alone wear them all regularly. Then an awful thing happened—her foot grew a size! (This happens occasionally to the best of us.) No longer do any of those hundreds of pairs of shoes fit her.

Like most women, I have a weakness for pretty shoes. But years ago I decided I didn't want to become a shoe-aholic, spending limited clothing funds on compulsive shoe-gratification. I wanted to have a neat closet. I wanted to know how many shoes I owned, and I wanted to wear them all, rather than letting them grow cobwebs in the dark recesses of my closet. So I purchased two shoe racks and allowed myself only as many shoes as I could fit on those two racks. If I bought a new pair, another pair had to go.

As a result, I rarely buy a new pair of shoes today. But when I do, I look for shoes that are very versatile in colors that can be worn with a lot of things in my closet, rather than glitzy, faddish styles. I also find that having fewer pairs of shoes makes it easier for me to keep them polished and in good condition, making them last longer. Since I don't buy a lot of shoes, I'm not forced to shop for a bargain every time. I hate paying full price for anything, but if I must do so to get just the right thing, at least I'm sure to get my money's worth.

This attitude about shoes has become my attitude about my entire wardrobe. I'm a great believer that, with wise purchasing, less is more. As women who desire to be faithful stewards of our finances and attractive representatives of Christ, we must continually exercise wisdom in achieving balance between too much and too little. And it is a constant challenge!

The closet-organizing business is booming in America today because we're trying to stuff too many unnecessary things into our closets and into our homes. (I've seen the tiny closets that our grandparents' generation had, and it makes me ashamed!)

Shopping has become a dangerous national pastime, tempting us to want much more than we need. We are then tempted to leave our homes for careers to finance our credit cards. Our families become consumer-oriented rather than home-centered. Meanwhile, we spend a fortune to "dress for success," all the while yearning for the good old days when we were homemakers who were content to wear jeans and a sweatshirt. It's one thing to go to work because we've made a deliberate decision to do so, but quite another to find ourselves stuck in a job we really didn't want just to pay for things we really didn't need!

So, go ahead and make that "want list," but don't let it rule your life. Good things come to those who wait, as they say. As a result of your sensible planning, when those things do come, you know they will be right for you. And you'll take care of them and make them last.

Meanwhile, you can enjoy the freedom that comes from simplicity. No longer are you bogged down with stressful clutter. All your clothes look great on you, and you know that they are ready to go when you are. Best of all, you look like a very classy lady, because you have one really classy closet!

Action Assignments

1. Select a day that you can spend cleaning out your closet. Write it on the calendar. Arrange for babysitting if needed.

2. Make a shopping list and purchase needed supplies before your "closet experience."

3. On the appointed day, clean out your closet using Phase I: emptying and cleaning; Phase II: trying on and sorting out; and Phase III: planning future acquisitions.

4. Make a "want list" of items you need to round out your wardrobe. Plan wisely, then stick to your plan. Keep that list in your personal notebook.

5. If you want to learn to sew, call your local fabric shops or community college for information on classes.

Suggested Reading

Jackson, Carole. *Color Me Beautiful.* New York: Ballantine Books, 1981.

Wallace, Joanne. *Dress to Fit Your Personality.* Old Tappan, NJ: Fleming H. Revell, 1989.

7

Are Our Hours Ours?

Carl Sandburg said, "Time is the coin of your life. It is the only coin you have, and only you can determine how it will be spent. Be careful lest you let other people spend it for you." Effective time management is the art of taking charge of how you spend your time.

We are all given the same amount of time each week. But what we accomplish with those 168 hours varies widely from person to person. Each of us has different things we want to, need to, and must accomplish with our time. Wise time management, which is crucial to achieving these goals, makes the difference between the achiever and the person who just muddles through life.

Priority Management Pittsburgh, Inc., a time management firm, has estimated that the average person spends eight months of his life opening junk mail, a year of his life searching for misplaced items, and five years waiting in line. These aren't things for which we'll receive crowns of glory in heaven—so why not manage our time more effectively?

The best time management tool in the world is learning to say no. Do not say yes to anything that you do not want to do. If you are not yet assertive enough to smile and say that little word unflinchingly, I suggest that you at least learn to say, "Let me think about it. I'll get back to you." Then get up your nerve to say no later. I estimate that this habit alone can save the average homemaker twenty-seven years. Another great time saver is to abstain from the following bad habits: watching television, reading junk literature, spending aimless hours on the telephone, and cleaning things that aren't dirty.

One formidable time waster is the habit of living from crisis to crisis. People who are controlled by the tyranny of the urgent are usually people who do not plan. Having a personal datebook will do wonders toward correcting that problem.

Creating Your Datebook

The most important step to take in managing your time is to manage yourself. The first step you can take to manage yourself is to have a datebook with which you plan your days. Keep this datebook in your purse. The only time it is to be out of your purse is when you're home. Then you'll want to refer to it often. If you have a datebook that's tailored to your own personal needs and you use it daily, it will liberate you from the tyranny of time pressure.

Stores carry dozens of different datebooks to help manage the busy lives of the career man or woman. I've found most of these daily planners to be useless to the career homemaker. You don't need to keep track of customers, business expenses, or mileage. You don't need to know what time it is in Japan or Europe. You *do* need to know which child needs to be carpooled at what time, when it's your turn to bake cookies for the Brownies, and what size your furnace filter is when you're standing in front of them at the store. I suggest you read the following requirements for an effective career homemaker's datebook before rushing out to purchase one. After selecting the specific components that you want in your personal datebook, you may decide it's more cost-effective to make your own by purchasing individual items rather than paying for one of those expensive career datebooks.

Over the years I've learned that a datebook must be large enough to accommodate a lot of information and yet small enough to fit into my purse. If it can't fit into my purse, I find that I never have it with me when I need it—which is always. It's too difficult to carry both a purse and a notebook, and it's too easy to lose your datebook carrying it separately. I refuse to carry a purse the size of a saddlebag just so my datebook can fit inside. I have finally settled on a small three-ring binder that is 5 inches by 7 inches. It holds notebook paper that is 3 3/4 inches by 6 3/4 inches. You can easily find this size of notebook paper in stores without having to search for an odd-sized, expensive paper created just for one particular brand of datebook.

Your datebook binder should have pockets inside the covers for holding a small calculator and a pen. I suggest you also purchase a clear plastic zip-lock pocket (like the kind your children put inside their large three-ring binders for pens, etc.) to hold small pieces of paper, such as the dry cleaner's receipt or a prescription that you need to get filled. If your datebook also has clear plastic three-ring inserts that hold credit cards and photos, you won't even need to carry a wallet. A small zippered money purse is all you'll need.

Organize Each Section

Whether you have those "luxury features" or not, you must have the sections that actually help you control your time. The first of those sections is your month-at-a-glance calendar, which must be purchased to fit in your particular notebook. This is a two-page monthly calendar with spaces for each day of the month that are large enough for you to write in appointments. Having a monthly calendar that's too small to write on only wastes space in your datebook. Because I want to see the whole month when I'm scheduling my activities, I've found that week-at-a-glance calendars are too confining. On this calendar write in such things as "3:00 p.m. Bobby to dentist," or "10:30 a.m. hair appointment."

Develop the habit of looking at this calendar every morning before you jump into your day, and you won't forget another appointment. Better yet, you won't schedule yourself to be in three different places at one time. When your friend asks, "Can you take my turn at carpooling next Thursday?" you whip out your monthly calendar (which is always with you for such moments) and reply, "Sorry, I have another appointment that day." It gives you a great sense of power to discover that no one argues with a woman who has a datebook!

The next important section of your datebook is the daily "To Do" section. This can contain pre-printed dated pages, or you can make your own pages from lined notebook paper with a different sheet for each day of the month. Write down everything you want to get done on a particular day in addition to the appointments that are written on your monthly calendar. You may have entries like "Plan for Saturday's dinner party"; "Get car repaired"; or "Return books to library." If you're lucky, some days may not have any entries at all, and others may have quite a lot. Your daily "To Do" list can show you if you are over-scheduling yourself. If you've written down 53 things to do on a single day, you know why you're feeling pressured and where to make some changes.

The best approach to accomplishing the things on your daily "To Do" list is to do the most important thing first, the second most important thing next, and so forth. The best way to decide which item is most important is to ask yourself, "Which one of these things will I be most happy tomorrow that I did today?" Then finish each item in order of importance before going on to the next. If you get only one thing checked off your list today, that's fine. Better one thing than nothing. And it was the most important thing you could have done, right? At the end of the day review your list, scratching off those tasks you accomplished. Simply re-schedule those things you didn't get done. Your daily "To Do" list eliminates worry, confusion, and guilt.

Behind the next divider in my datebook, labeled "Notes," I keep blank lined paper. It's nice to have a piece of paper handy for jotting down information or taking impromptu notes. I've labeled the next section in my datebook "To Buy." This is my ongoing "want list"—things I don't need to rush right out and buy today, but want to remember to purchase as soon as I have the extra time and money to get them.

Right now my list includes "new 60 x 90 drapes for Scot's room," "bluejean skirt," "flower arrangement for coffee table," and "hairbands." This list also comes in handy whenever my husband or my mother asks, "What would you like for your birthday?" I used to go blank and say, "Oh, I don't know." (Can you ever think of something good when they ask you?) Now I whip out my "want list" and say, "Well, there's a certain blouse at Dillard's that I've had my eye on." Why not use your want list to help someone else with his gift list?

The next section of your datebook should be labeled "Misc." You'll record certain information here that just doesn't fit anywhere else. This is the perfect place to write down the size of your furnace filters, for example. One page lists the sizes I need for tablecloths. On another page I wrote down what type of typewriter ribbon my typewriter needs. Have you ever forgotten the model number when you get to the store? I'm sure you can think of similar things that would be helpful to you.

The last section to put into your datebook is the "Gifts" section discussed in Chapter 8, unless you don't have enough room in your datebook. Then you may want to make a separate, smaller notebook for that purpose.

As you can see, a personal datebook is a lifesaver for the woman who is serious about controlling her time and enjoying her life. You can make it exactly like the one that I've described, or you can design it according to your own personal needs. The only important thing is that you make it!

Cultivating a Quiet Time

Having a daily, morning "quiet time" with God is essential for the woman who wishes to have a calm, directed day. I have practiced the discipline of a daily quiet time, with only occasional lapses, for fifteen years. I can assure you that it's the most important discipline you can practice. The days that I've rushed into action without pausing for those precious minutes of prayer and solitude have convinced me of their importance—I am invariably disorganized and distraught before the day is over. That's why I don't often forget!

How long should your quiet time be? That depends on how much you want to benefit from it. A little time yields a little benefit. More time yields more benefit. The benefits are not only those that can be immediately seen or felt, although there are those. The major benefit of having a daily quiet time is a cumulative one. After many days, weeks, and months of sitting at the Master's feet, listening to His voice, and meditating on His Word, you are changed. You will take on a deeper peace, wisdom, and confidence.

You can't help becoming more like Jesus after giving Him the prime moments of your day, day after day. You'll find yourself communing more with Him throughout the day, having established a close relationship each morning. After a while you find yourself speaking to Him whenever a problem or a decision arises. You ask Him to help you shop wisely as you enter the grocery store. In short, you begin to practice the presence of Christ in your moment to moment life. This alone is worth taking the time to sit at His feet when you are tempted to hurry on to other things.

I suggest that your quiet time be early in the morning, rather than later in the day or in the evening. King David repeatedly referred to his morning prayers, saying, "In the morning, O Lord, Thou wilt hear my voice; in the morning I will order my prayer to Thee and eagerly watch" (Psalm 5:3). It only makes sense that we offer God, the Giver and Sustainer of life, the firstfruits of our day.

It's also best to get into the Word before you get into the world. Once you get busy in your worldly affairs, time has a way of slipping by. How much better it is to cover yourself, your family, and your daily affairs with prayer for God's protection and guidance before springing into action. I've found this such an indispensable help that when I was working the 7:00 a.m. shift as a nurse, I set my alarm clock for 4:45 a.m. just to be sure I had time for my quiet time before going to work. Our work as homemakers is no less needy of God's provision.

Whenever I have my quiet time, there are always three books at my side. The first, of course, is my Bible. The second is my datebook, described previously in this chapter. That may sound funny until you think about it. My datebook has all my day's plans written in it. I can pray over them as I have my quiet time. If anything else I need to do comes to my mind (some people call them distractions), I just quickly jot it down in my datebook and proceed with my prayers. Perhaps I remember that I should phone someone, or drop a card to a sick friend on my prayer list. Perhaps I remember that I need to schedule an appointment to get the car fixed. By the time I finish my quiet time, my day is planned.

The third book that I have with me during my quiet time is what I call my "quiet time notebook." This is something that I have developed over the years to help me in my prayers and meditations, and I would have a difficult time trying to pray without it. It is a standard size, loose-leaf notebook with lined paper and dividers. Inside the front cover is a zippered pocket where I keep a pen. Then I have several helpful sections.

1. Schedules
   - Daily
   - Weekly
   - Monthly
2. Journal
3. Prayers
4. Miscellaneous

Being able to refer to each section during my quiet time has done wonders for my life. Let's look at each one.

Schedules

I've labeled the first section "Schedules." The first page in that section outlines my goals. I've heard it said that, "She who fails to plan, plans to fail." I believe that. If you don't have any goals, you surely won't achieve them. If you don't have your goals written down, you surely won't remember them. And if you don't look at them often, you surely won't accomplish them.

If you don't have your goals written down, be sure to do that during your next quiet time. Make it a matter of prayer and serious thought. How do you want to change over the next year? Do you want to grow spiritually? Write that down. How, specifically, do you plan to achieve that goal? Perhaps you want to have a daily quiet time. If so, write that below your major heading of "Spiritual Growth." Perhaps you want to read a chapter a day in the Bible. Maybe you want to join a Bible study or serve others through some type of ministry. Write those goals down.

Perhaps your next major goal is to "Get Organized." If so, write your sub-goals below that, such as, "Clean out the closets," or "Make a datebook." Write your goals, and then look at those goals every morning during your quiet time. Pray for wisdom in your priorities, and you'll begin to know what to tackle first and what to leave for later.

Daily Schedule

Behind your goals write your daily schedule, such as when you will wake up, when you will have your quiet time, when you will exercise, and when you will spend time with your family. What time will you go to bed? (The secret to rising early is going to bed early!) What part of each day will you devote to daily chores? If you're fresh in the morning, schedule your mornings as your work time. If you do better later in the day, schedule afternoons as daily chore time.

I encourage you not to do daily chores (laundry, ironing, housework, etc.) during the evenings if your husband is home then. Just as your husband accomplishes his work and the children go to school (which is their work), the time for a homemaker to accomplish her work is also during the day. This allows time for family togetherness in the evenings.

Why else do you want to be a homemaker but to have your evenings free to be with your family? This is one luxury most women with full-time, away-from-home jobs do not have. As a career homemaker you can arrange your schedule any way you want—so why not take advantage of this opportunity? Make evenings family time: dinner, talking, reading and studying, taking walks, or whatever your family enjoys most. This is your special time to nurture your loved ones, which you can't do if you're busy doing what you could have done during the day. This is your time to develop a love of home in your family.

Weekly Schedule

On the next page write your weekly household chores schedule. Having a master schedule to plan your work adds so much more order in your life. If you want to juggle days around occasionally, that's fine. But having a plan relieves you of time-wasting decision making and uncertainty. It frees you to get the work done quickly while someone else is still trying to decide what to do today. Your plan can also change as your children grow older, allowing you larger blocks of time and greater flexibility. This weekly schedule isn't written in stone, but it won't work for you unless you write it down and use it. Here's a sample weekly schedule that works well for many students who take my homemaker's class:

Monday: Laundry, ironing, mending. Straighten drawers and closets as you put away the clean clothes. Wash the sheets and put them back on the beds. Attend to mending so it won't pile up.

Tuesday: Clean the house. (See Chapter 2.)

Wednesday: Grocery shopping and errands. Schedule all elective doctor and dentist appointments for this day. Buy gas and drive through the car wash. Be sure to take your "Errand Bag" along. (See Chapter 4.)

Thursday: Special Projects Day. What are your special monthly goals? Use this day to do the things you always wished you had time to do: re-organize the photo albums and your recipes, or start some of the projects in this book. Accomplish fun things on this day. (See Chapter 3.)

Friday: Free Day! This is your day to spend on yourself! If you ever take the children to Grandma's house, this is the day to do it! Then give yourself a manicure. Get your hair done. Attend a Bible study. Go to the art museum. Have lunch with a friend. Are you getting the idea?

Saturday: Yardwork and gardening day in the summer. Baking or sewing day in the winter. Remember that chore time should take up only half of the day. Use the other half of the day to do something fun as a family! In good weather you can go swimming or to the zoo. In poor weather make a trek to the library and check out some books and videos.

Sunday: The Lord's Day. Go to church. Take a nap in the afternoon. Create an atmosphere of quiet restfulness in your home. Why not cook enough food on Saturday to last through Sunday, or have your big meal at a restaurant and serve sandwiches at home? Save your entertaining for Friday or Saturday nights if you want to rest on Sunday.

Monthly Schedule

Your last schedule page can be your list of monthly "Special Projects" discussed in Chapter 3. This is the perfect place to keep it. On the first cleaning day of every month, change the furnace filter and the sweeper bag. Here's an example of monthly Special Projects goals for the entire year:

January:	Clean the basement or attic. (Isn't it always a mess after putting away the Christmas decorations?)
February:	Deep clean your office and files. (See Chapter 5.)
March:	Deep clean the kitchen.
April:	Deep clean the master bedroom and closet.
May:	Deep clean bedroom #2.
June:	Deep clean bedroom #3.
July:	Deep clean the family room.
August:	Deep clean the laundry room. Back-to-school shopping. Schedule family medical and dental check-ups. Have family photo taken for Christmas cards.
September:	Deep clean bathroom and linen closets.
October:	Deep clean living room, entry room, and clothes closet.
November:	Deep clean dining room. (You'll be ready for holiday entertaining.)
December:	Bake cookies, decorate, and enjoy Christmas!

Be sure to look at the "Schedules" section of your notebook every morning during your quiet time to refresh your memory and strengthen your resolve.

Journal

The second section of your quiet time notebook could be labeled "Journal." Here I write my thoughts to God every day. Some days it's just meaningless drivel to anyone other than myself, like what I did yesterday, or what kind of weather we're having. Other days my journal contains heart-wrenching prayers or psalms of praise. It's quite a potpourri of thoughts that I've written over the past fifteen years, and it's rather fun to reflect upon occasionally. One important note on keeping a journal is to be sure your family knows to keep out; it is strictly your personal book. Be careful not to write any specifics that could be hurtful to someone else if it were read by another.

If you feel overwhelmed by the thought of keeping a daily journal, why not set a more attainable goal? Perhaps you could write two or three entries a week. Record the highlights of your life: insights into Scripture, opportunities to minister, or an encouraging word that God whispers to you in prayer. What godly aspirations has He deposited in your heart? Do you remember the last direction God gave you? Write it down! Your journal will help you to become more diligent in fulfilling God's will for your life.

Prayers

The third section of your quiet time notebook is for recording your prayers. I like to pray for different subjects each day of the week. My Monday prayer list focuses on immediate family, my Tuesday prayer list concentrates on extended family and special requests, and so forth. By the end of the week you will have found time to pray for your church, the government, and the world.

Write your prayer list however you like, but write it. How else will you know when God answers your prayers unless you remember what you prayed? When the answer comes, just cross it off, date it, and write "P.T.L.!" You have a permanent record of events to thank God for. Your prayer list will also remind you of God's faithfulness when you're feeling low.

Miscellaneous

The following sections can hold information on anything that interests you. In one section I write down goals for fixing up my house. I also keep records of previous home improvements. Another section contains records of guests I've entertained, what menu I served, and the date. This list comes in handy when I need ideas for parties and luncheons. Another section lists books that I've read. Use your imagination and come up with ideas that are tailored to your own personality and walk with the Lord.

This section of your notebook can be devoted to saving notes from sermons and seminars that you have attended. (I keep notebook paper, folded in half, inside the cover of my Bible for this purpose.) If this or any other section gets too bulky after a while, you may want to transfer some of its contents to a file folder and put it in your file cabinet. (See Chapter 5.)

As you can see, a quiet time notebook is an invaluable tool in helping you to discipline yourself in your personal goals. The more you use it, the more it blesses you.

Managing Your Minutes

Most of the time that we waste is not in large blocks but rather in small fragments. Like sand, productive minutes can slip, unused, through our fingertips. To avoid this, we must redeem those little nonproductive moments that meander

through our day. We often waste our small moments because
we think they're useless. But every sixty-second interval is
just as useful as another, whether it is joined with others
to form an hour or not.

We also waste our minutes because we think it takes longer
to complete most tasks than it really does. That's why we
concentrated on watching the clock while doing housework
in Chapter 2. Most women are surprised to discover that
it only takes three minutes to make a bed, and that they can
do all their housework much more quickly than they
thought. One woman in my homemaker's class said, "I can't
believe how much time I've wasted all my life because I
believed it took so long to do housework. The first time I
concentrated on just cleaning the house while watching the
clock, I learned that I could clean my entire two-story house
in just two and a half hours. I had never done that before!"

If being aware of time can help us accomplish big jobs,
it certainly can help us to accomplish a multitude of little
jobs as well. The following list of small tasks can be completed in those short, idle moments we spend on such things
as waiting for the microwave to finish heating, talking on
the telephone, or waiting for the dog to come back inside.

- Clean a kitchen drawer
- Empty the dishwasher
- Scour the sink
- Sew on a button
- Wash fresh vegetables
- File nails
- Clip coupons
- Fix a lunch
- Sort through the mail
- Wipe off the cabinets
- Read a recipe
- Organize a kitchen shelf
- Say a prayer

To make good use of those idle moments away from home, always take something with you when you leave the house. You can balance your checkbook while waiting at the doctor's office, work on a quilt while sitting through Little League practice, or read a book on money management while your daughter has her braces adjusted. If you forget to take something to do, you can use those spare moments to pray for your family, your friends, or for strangers around you. That is certainly productive. Let not a moment escape your grasp that you don't use intentionally, whether to accomplish something or to relax tired muscles and breathe deeply. The secret is to be fully conscious of your minutes. That's what life on earth is made of. Don't let it slip away!

Action Assignments

1. Practice responding to demands on your time by saying, "I'll think about it—let me get back to you."
2. Make a datebook.
3. Begin a daily quiet time, even if it is only fifteen minutes.
4. Make a quiet time notebook.
5. Practice being consciously aware of the value of each minute.

8

Gracious Gift Giving

The doorbell rings unexpectedly. When you answer it, you're surprised to see your friend Frieda standing there looking a bit distraught.

"Come on in, Frieda," you say, holding the door open.

"Oh, I can't stay, honey, I'm so busy. Just wanted to drop off this present for you," she gushes as she shoves a crumpled paper sack at you. "I know your birthday was a month ago, but I forgot all about it. Sorry I didn't have time to wrap it or get a card, but it's the thought that counts, right? I hope it fits—I had to guess at your size." As she heads back toward her car she calls out, "I've got to rush, darling. Let's do lunch soon, shall we? Happy birthday!"

You close the door and look forlornly at the paper sack in your hands. A peek inside reveals a beautiful sweater. True, it's not your size. True, it doesn't look a bit like you. But Frieda obviously spent a mint on this sweater. So why aren't you feeling too excited about this gift? And why aren't you feeling too excited about Frieda's friendship, either?

Then you remember how differently you felt when Susan gave you a birthday gift. It was just a little gift, a pretty sachet for your bureau drawer. But you felt so special the way Susan treated you that day. She invited you over for lunch on her back porch. You enjoyed a pleasant visit together, sipping lemonade and nibbling finger sandwiches. Then she gave you that little package all tied up in colored paper and fussy ribbons, with a touching card that she had made herself. Now whenever you see that little sachet in your drawer or smell its sweet scent, you remember a happy afternoon spent with a devoted friend.

No, it wasn't the gift that pointed out the difference between these two friends—it was the manner in which the gift was given. Truly, the way a gift is given says much more than the gift itself. And it says a whole lot more about the gift giver.

A gift thoughtlessly given—no matter how expensive— says loud and clear, "This is the best I cared to do for you." But a gift given graciously says, "You are so special that I took the time and effort to tell you so." Isn't that the whole purpose of gift giving—to make a person feel special? When we give out of obligation or habit, rather than thoughtfulness, the effect is just the opposite.

Of course, all of us have been caught short at one time or another when it comes to gracious gift giving. But has sloppy gift giving become a habit, or is it an exception to our usual thoughtfulness? We don't want to fall into the pattern of some people who always act like birthdays and Christmas have caught them totally by surprise—as if they had no idea that these things always happen on the same day every year.

It isn't out of intentional thoughtlessness or carelessness that we become guilty of such things. It is simply because of over-busy, under-organized lives. The cure is to take a few hours and concentrate on correcting these problems. Knowing that every effort invested now in planning and organizing our gift giving will pay off in many smiles when those gifts are given, let us begin. To become a gracious gift giver, you need to take the following five steps.

1. Make a gift budget.
2. Make a gift notebook.
3. Shop in advance.
4. Give creative rather than expensive gifts.
5. Make a gift center.

Let's look at each one in more detail.

Make a Gift Budget

Write the name of the recipient, the occasion, and the date for every gift you plan to give over the next year. Include friends, relatives, and anyone else you give gifts to each year. Be sure to make allowance for a couple of unexpected gift giving occasions, such as weddings, graduations, or new babies. Are you shocked at the length of your list? (If not, you'd probably better figure again.)

Review your list and see if there are any changes you should make. Are there any gifts that you're giving perfunctorily? Is it just a tradition that you send Aunt Fran a box of candy every year, and she sends you one in return? How about just exchanging cards instead? If you have a large family, could you suggest name-drawing at Christmas or setting a price limit on each gift? Could you agree to limit gift exchanging to the children and let the adults exchange hugs and cookies?

Try to eliminate all gift giving that is done out of obligation alone. The Bible tells us that we are to give "not grudgingly or under compulsion; for God loves a cheerful giver" (2 Corinthians 9:7). God also wants us to be wise stewards of our resources. Pray over each entry, asking for discernment and wisdom.

Once you have tightened up your gift list, you may want to consider adding some new names. Are there any people that you appreciate for their special kindnesses throughout the year? A kind mailman? A favorite checker at the grocery store? Have you noticed an elderly shut-in who never seems to have a visitor? You can brighten someone's life with a small, unexpected token of your appreciation or friendship at any time of the year. Perhaps your family would like to make a gift box during the holidays for a needy family. Once you've eliminated the time and expense of pointless gift giving, you can plan these special acts of kindness.

Once you've made your gift list, then comes the hard part—determining a monetary limit for each gift. You and your husband need to decide exactly how much you wish to allot to your yearly gift fund. Then determine how you want to slice that pie. Do not be influenced by what other people spend. Decide how much you will spend on birthday gifts, on Christmas gifts, and other gifts. Don't forget to include the expense of purchasing gift cards, wrapping paper, ribbons, and postage. Put your gift budget in writing, and then write the monetary limit behind each entry on your list. Then stick to that budget. A budget won't benefit you if you don't use it faithfully.

Make a Gift Notebook

This can be a small, separate notebook, or it can be a separate section of your purse notebook. (See Chapter 7.) Your gift notebook consists of three sections. Make the first section a yearly perpetual calendar where you write the dates of every occasion for which you need to give a gift or send a card. This section always stays the same, except for occasional corrections or additions. You can make this calendar yourself by taking twelve sheets of paper and writing a different month on the top of each page. Then on separate lines write the numbers 1 through 31 underneath the month. Fill in the name and occasion on the appropriate lines, such as "Susan's birthday" on June 3. Remember to include reminders of Mother's Day, Father's Day, and any other annual holiday you observe.

In the second section of your notebook, have a separate page for each person on your gift list. Put the person's name on the top of the page. Below that write the dates of when you give gifts or cards to that person, such as their birthday or Christmas. Behind each occasion write the amount of money that you budgeted for that person on that occasion. Below that write down all pertinent gift-giving information such as sizes of clothing, favorite colors, decor of rooms in the home, special interests, etc. Use the space below that to jot down any gift-giving ideas that you may think of during the year. If you don't write it down immediately, you probably won't remember that idea when you go shopping. All this information goes on the front of each sheet of paper.

On the backside of these pages, write the following headings: "Date," "Occasion," "Item," and "Price." Every time you purchase a gift, fill in the information in the appropriate column below these headings. This will serve as a permanent record of gifts that you have given each person, as well as a record of your gift expenses. Be sure to save every receipt in your receipt box. (See Chapter 4.)

The third section of your gift notebook is a current yearly gift needs list. At the beginning of each year take some clean sheets of paper and, starting with January, list in chronological order each gift and card that you need to give this year. So you may have "January 6, Mom and Dad's anniversary. Send Card." Your next entry may be "February 21. Tom's birthday. Gift and card," and so forth throughout the year. Leave a space behind each entry to check off when you have purchased the card or gift. You'll have an instant, up-to-date record of what you need and what you have already obtained. If you include your Christmas gifts on this list, you can be doing your Christmas shopping all year.

Keep your gift notebook in your purse because you never know when you'll need it. The next time you come across a great sale, you can flip open your notebook, see exactly what your gift needs are, and take advantage of the sale. You won't get stuck wondering, Did I get Jane a birthday gift yet? or What size blouse does Grandma wear? Everything you need to know is at your fingertips.

Shop in Advance

How many of us have allowed last minute shopping to take all the fun out of Christmas? And how many of us have an excuse for that, knowing that Christmas is coming again, barring the Lord's return? The same is true of birthdays, anniversaries, and most other gift-giving occasions. So why wait until the heat is on to shop? Last-minute shopping leads to poor gift selection, gross over-spending, and minor nervous breakdowns. Ever notice how the closer it gets to Christmas, the more sour the expressions on the faces of shoppers? They are obviously not enjoying the spirit of Christmas.

At a seminar my husband and I once attended, Gary Smalley, instructor and author, stated that one of the major differences between most men and women is in their shopping habits. Men, he said, are natural "hunters," while women are into "experiences." When most men shop they are subconsciously seeking to fulfill that urge to "hunt" their prey, sack it, and quickly drag it home. Women, on the other hand, usually prefer shopping to be a pleasant "experience'—perhaps an all-afternoon event that includes enjoying sights, sounds, smells, conversations, and even lunch with a friend. (This explains why my husband and I are not compatible shoppers!)

But whatever kind of shopper you are, last-minute shopping can turn you into a grouchy, desperate "hunter," unable to experience any of the satisfactions that a composed shopping trip can bring. The major advantage of shopping in advance is that it is more economical, allowing you to compare wisely and to take advantage of sales. Whenever

I'm tempted to buy something at full price, my husband says, "Everything is on sale sometime." He's absolutely right. So why not purchase items that are marked down, rather than marked up? How often have you rushed out to buy a gift and found just the right thing on sale? Never? It seems that the greater the pressure to buy, the higher the price. Shop early and beat the system. You'll enjoy yourself in the process.

Give Creative Gifts

Emerson said, "Rings and jewels are not gifts but apologies for gifts. The only true gift is a portion of thyself." A creative gift is a portion of yourself. It need not be expensive, only unique—contoured to the person being gifted. Anyone can walk into a store with a credit card and do a year's worth of shopping at one time. But a creative gift says, "I went to the trouble to think of something special for you."

A creative gift might be a snapshot of you and your friend at the zoo. It could be a mugful of assorted teabags. It might be something that only you knew the person would like to have. So why give the usual fare? Why not give your sports-loving brother a ticket to the baseball game in a new baseball cap? Take your niece, who is learning to play the violin, to an orchestra performance. Deep clean the inside of your husband's car. Teach a friend how to knit. Or babysit for a neighbor so she can do her Christmas shopping.

A creative gift can also be a handmade gift. Receiving a token of your invested time and talent makes a person feel very special. One of the fringe benefits of being a full-time homemaker is that we can take the time to develop our creativity and then use that talent as a gift to others. Handmade gifts are the greatest fun to give. Some that I have given in the past are ceramic geese and Christmas trees, crocheted caps and scarves, knitted golf club covers, embroidered pictures, home-sewn tablecloths and matching placemats, and home-baked cookies served on an attractive garage-sale dish.

If you "don't know how to make a thing," don't despair—
you can learn! Most communities have craft classes in adult
evening schools. Sewing centers offer sewing classes for a
nominal fee. You'll flatter relatives by asking, "Could you
teach me how to do that?" (I learned to crochet from my
husband's Great Aunt Minnie.) Last year I learned how to
make pretty ladies' collars and placemats at a women's
church group. I also took a quilting class at a local quilt shop.
You can find endless craft ideas in the books at your library.
The opportunities for learning are endless once you start
looking. Never pass up an opportunity to learn a new skill.
It is something you can use, and something you can teach
to your children.

Make your gift projects a family affair by including your
children in the process. You will be teaching them the value
of giving while teaching them skills. And you will be creating family memories while creating gifts.

Encourage your children to make greeting cards. Our sons
became quite talented at making personalized cards for any
occasion. Now that they are grown young men, I like to get
out the memorabilia box and look at the sweet and funny
cards they made over the years for their father and me. Many
of our relatives have their own similar collections of Scot
and Todd creations tucked away where store-bought cards
would have been long forgotten. Creative gifts are a blessing to the recipient and to the giver as well.

Make a Gift Center

A gift center is a place where you keep all your gift wrapping supplies in one convenient spot. It can be as simple
as a cardboard, under-bed storage box, or as elaborate as a
big walk-in closet (for those of you fortunate enough to have
a spare one handy.) My gift center consists of an old table
next to a set of shelves in the basement. I use the table for
wrapping and the shelves for storing my supplies and gifts.

I love my gift center because I never have to go scrounging through the house to find giftwrap, tape, or scissors.

To make your own gift center you will need the following supplies:

- Giftwrap (Save the Sunday comics for wrapping children's gifts.)
- Tissue for lining boxes
- Boxes
- Cellophane tape
- Ribbons and bows
- Scissors
- Ink pen
- Greeting cards
- Brown mailing paper and tape
- Trash can

When you have made a nice present or have shopped in advance with the help of your gift notebook, you will actually look forward to wrapping it in your gift center. Attach a pretty bow and card and set it on the shelf, ready to go. Then when that occasion comes you will feel confident and gracious. Best of all, the person you are "gifting" will, indeed, feel special. Remember, it's not important how much you give but rather how much love you put in the giving.

Action Assignments

1. Make a yearly gift budget.
2. Make a gift notebook.
3. Make a gift center.
4. Think of some creative gifts you can give.

9

Feeding Your Family

"The worst thing about being a homemaker is having to fix breakfast, lunch, and dinner every day, day in and day out," sighed Maggie. "It's an endless, thankless task. And it seems that the more time I spend trying to make a new and different meal, the more complaints I get about it!"

I knew just what she meant. I'll never forget when I was a young bride, trying to learn to cook things that pleased my husband. He liked chili, so I consulted several different recipes in an attempt to find one he liked. After I spent hours simmering some fancy concoction of ingredients, Mark sat down, took a careful taste, and said, "Well—it's okay, but it just doesn't taste like my mother's chili."

Finally I bought a can of chili, heated it on the stove, and sat it before him to see if he would appreciate the difference. This time when Mark took a bite, his eyes got big and a wide grin spread across his face.

"Well, honey," he said, "you finally did it. This tastes just like Mom's!"

Today I can laugh at that story, but at the time I didn't think it was a bit funny. But the more I got to know my mother-in-law, the more I learned from her that doing things the hard way isn't always necessarily the best way. That's especially true in the kitchen.

When it comes to getting meals on the table, the homemaker has a choice: she can look at this duty as a dreary chore, or she can look at it as an opportunity for creative ministry to her family. The disorganized homemaker will probably approach it as the former. The organized homemaker is more likely to approach it as the latter. Organization makes all the difference in how successful we are at providing healthy, enjoyable meals for our families.

To be organized in this area of homemaking, we need to concentrate on several inter-related areas:

1. Organization in the kitchen
2. Menu planning
3. Shopping
4. Meal preparation

Let's look at each one in detail. By following these practical tips, you won't have to dread feeding your family.

Organization in the Kitchen

If you were a famous cook, such as Julia Childs or Martha Stewart, would you be satisfied with the organization of your kitchen? You probably don't have—or need—the large assortment of equipment that those women have. Perhaps you dream of having a large, up-to-date kitchen like they do. But one thing that you can have just as much as any famous cook is a well-organized, smoothly functioning kitchen.

Since feeding your family every day is just as important as cooking for books and television shows, you need an organized kitchen just as much as they do. And, as a busy wife and mother, your time and personal satisfaction are just as valuable as theirs. But, just like Julia and Martha, you alone can organize your kitchen in a manner that is just right for you. So, taking into account your own kitchen layout and your personal cooking habits, begin by taking a critical look at your kitchen.

Here are two important organizational tips that will streamline your kitchen:

1. Get rid of everything you don't use.
2. Group similar items together.

Search all cabinets, drawers, and the pantry for freeloaders that take up space without paying their way. If you've had that fondue pot for ten years only to dust it once a year and replace it on the shelf, put it in a large box labeled "Get Out of My Kitchen!" Put anything and everything that you do not use into that box. Then give that box away or put it in a garage sale. (No sneaking things back out later!) Get rid of anything you haven't used in the past year or two.

The only exception to this should be items that you never use only because they're so poorly stored that they've been too difficult to get out or you forget that you even have them. Now that you've made more space by throwing out items that you don't need or want, put these seldom-used tools in a more convenient location. For instance, if you never use your food processor because it's stashed away in a deep, dark corner near the stove, you need to find it a better home. A food processor is a valuable tool for any cook. Wash it and make a place for it where it can be easily retrieved.

Do not keep equipment that does what another piece of equipment can do. When my blender broke, I didn't need to replace it because my food processor could do anything the blender could do, and more. Several small appliances that duplicate the same work may be stealing space in your kitchen.

Get rid of equipment that you don't use because it's too much work to clean after each use, or because it is just too specialized. Do you really use that hot dog cooker that your mother gave you for Christmas? Do you ever use that waffle iron? Or that fritter fryer? Or that noodle maker? If you haven't used it in the past year, you probably don't need it. If you want to start using it, make it more accessible.

Keep in mind that the fewer things you own, the less those things own you. Make it your goal to see how little, rather than how much, you can get by with. How many pots and pans do you have? How many burners are on your stove? If you have only four burners, do you really need thirty pots and pans? Ask yourself these questions as you weed through your kitchen.

Once you've finished your search-and-destroy mission, it's time to rearrange what remains. The key to quickly finding items in your kitchen is to group similar items together. For example, use each shelf in your food pantry for a different type of item. Perhaps the top shelf could be used to store paper items. The next shelf could be used to store baking items. The next could be used for boxed items. The next for canned items, and the next for glass bottles and jars. Whenever you put away groceries, you know exactly on which shelf to put them. When you're looking for an item, you know exactly where to find it.

Grouping items makes organization easy. Subgrouping makes it even easier. Organize your canned goods in neat rows so you know that whatever you can't see is the same as the can in front of it. Stack a row of canned string beans, a row of corn, a row of peas, and a row of soup from front to back on the shelf. Group the cake mixes in a row on the boxed goods shelf, then group the boxes of pasta, etc. If you have a lot of spices, arrange them alphabetically so you don't have to search. When you buy new spices, mark them with the date and replace them in a year so they'll always be fresh.

Follow the same idea in your cabinets. Keep all metal pots and pans in one area. Group all plastic containers on another shelf. Store all your china in one place, all your plastic dishes in another. Keep all your drinking glasses in one place and all your baking items in another. If you have the room, you can make a baking center by storing all your baking bowls, utensils, and appliances in one convenient location. A center island is perfect for this.

Do the same thing in your kitchen drawers: have one drawer for tableware; another drawer for potholders, towels, and dishcloths; another drawer for utensils; and another drawer for paper, pencils, coupons, scissors, etc. Designate one box in your utensil drawer for metal utensils and another box for plastic ones. When you're looking for a particular utensil, you'll only need to root through half as much stuff. Keep all your cookbooks in one place.

Organize your freezer shelves in the same way—one shelf for beef, one for pork, one for fish, one for bread, and one for ice cubes and ice cream. Store vegetables on the door. Then do the same inside the refrigerator. Mark the shelves with masking tape labels to help you remember what goes where until you get used to your new system.

Instead of storing everything in your crowded cabinets or pantry, use a baker's rack or some attractive shelving. If there isn't enough room in the kitchen, consider storing seldom-used items in an adjacent room, such as the laundry room. Store pots and pans on a rack hanging from the ceiling or hang utensils on a rack over the stove. Use pretty plates, baskets, or tea pots as part of your decor by displaying them on shelves where you can easily retrieve them. Or put dishes that you use only for entertaining in the dining room. If there isn't enough room in your china cabinet, store those items in a basement cabinet, bringing them upstairs only as needed.

One more important area to organize is the open areas of your kitchen. Keep the absolute minimum of items on your countertops. Nothing is as dreary as a countertop with appliances crammed shoulder to shoulder like people in a crowded elevator. Allow only those items that are used every day, such as the toaster or the can opener, to sit on top of the counter. Put other items behind closed doors if possible.

Next, clear off the top of the refrigerator. That not only makes the kitchen more attractive, but makes it easier to dust once a week when you clean. Try to minimize the number of items stuck on the front of the refrigerator with magnets.

Remove as much decorative clutter from walls and exposed shelving as possible for a clean, crisp look. The fewer decorative items there are in any room, the more impact each piece has. It's better to have a few pretty serving pieces on a shelf than two dozen so-so pieces. "Less is more" applies to decorating as well as it does to many other areas of life.

Menu Planning

One way to avoid monotonous meals and high grocery bills is to plan your weekly menus before grocery shopping. Many women don't plan their menus because they don't want to search through stacks of cookbooks and clippings to get menu ideas. Why not make your own personal cookbook filled with your favorite recipes with a menu section in the front?

Using a large three-ring binder and notebook dividers, transfer your dependable family favorites to this notebook. Write them out on lined notebook paper, tape recipes clipped from newspapers on notebook paper, or photocopy your favorite recipes out of books or from recipe cards. Mark your dividers according to recipe categories such as "Beef," "Chinese," "Desserts," etc. If you don't want to make a three-ring binder, use a photo album with plastic self-adhesive pages to keep recipes from magazines, recipe cards, etc. This requires no re-copying of recipes.

In the front section list dinner menus that your family likes, striving to include a balanced, healthy selection of foods for each meal. When it's time to make your menus for the week, you can simply select from your already made-up assortment of menus. If you write one menu per page, you won't even have to write those menus down each week—just open your binder, pull out the menus you intend to use, and fasten them to your bulletin board or the side of the refrigerator. To make your shopping list, simply check the recipes in your notebook to see which ingredients you need to buy.

Find a set day of the week to select your weekly menus, clip coupons and check grocery store ads, write your grocery shopping list, and clean out the refrigerator. While you're restoring order to the shelves and throwing out any leftovers that are growing penicillin, you can easily see what items you need to buy. Straighten pantry shelves while checking for the same. All these activities work so well together that it only makes sense to do them at the same time. The best time to schedule these activities is the night before or the morning of your trip to the grocery store. When you get home with your groceries, your refrigerator and pantry will be orderly and relatively empty.

Grocery Shopping

Ideally, the wise homemaker never shops with children but instead leaves them home with her fairy godmother. For those of us who live in the real world, however, the following advice will help to eliminate the headaches and hassles of shopping with kids.

When you must shop with children, limit the time period that you're out. Plan your trip to the grocery store when your kids are rested and not hungry. If you have a toddler who may grow weary trudging down those long aisles, take a stroller. Let your older kids bring along a favorite book or toy. Be sure to establish the rules *before* you leave the house. Reinforce them in the car before you enter the store.

Getting through the store without causing a scene in front of the cookies or the latest sugar-coated cereal with a prize in the box is a challenge for any mother. I suggest you resort to bribery. Promise your kids a reward for good behavior. Allow them to pick one item *after* you go through the check-out. See if your store has a no-candy check-out line for mothers. If you must discipline your child for misbehaving, do it outside or when you return home—not in public.

Plan your grocery shopping for the same day each week according to your weekly schedule. (See Chapter 7.) Decide whether you want to shop at one convenient location or hunt bargains at several different grocery stores depending on your schedule, your energy level, and your budget.

I like what Jeff Smith says on his TV cooking show, *The Frugal Gourmet*. Whenever someone criticizes him for preparing an elegant dish, he replies, "Frugal doesn't mean cheap—it means you never waste anything!" That's true in grocery shopping, meal preparation, and every other area of homemaking.

In my early years of marriage I learned how to make a tiny grocery budget feed us all week. To this day I can't bear to throw out a perfectly good turkey carcass any more than I can resist saving every scrap of fabric for a quilt. Turning worthless leftovers into something valuable is an art.

A friend once told me, "You're the most frugal person I know." I took that as a compliment. As long as you don't confuse "frugal" with "cheap," it is an admirable quality. How can you keep from being too parsimonious? Be a giver who's always on the lookout for ways to bless others out of your however-limited abundance. Whenever guests visit, see if you can send them home with something. Give a friend a little gift of cookies or homemade soup. Then watch how God will bless you in return. One of the ways He will give back to you is by showing you new ideas on how to stretch your budget. Feeding your family wisely is one of the best ways you can do that.

Be sure to take your coupons and the weekly grocery store ads. Instead of carrying the whole newspaper full of ads, I clip out only those sale items I want to purchase and staple them together in the order that I'll come across them in the store. I don't save coupons for items that I don't really want just for the sake of saving a few cents. If you don't use it, it isn't a bargain. Even so, my coupons save a few dollars each week, which amounts to a worthwhile savings each year. And I don't spend time on refunding that requires me to save boxes and wrappers. If you have the time and patience for that, my compliments to you.

Never go grocery shopping on an empty stomach, or you'll surely buy too many doughnuts, cookies, and other tempting treats that put pounds on the hips and dollars on the cash register. The best grocery shopper sticks to her shopping list without deviating from it in the pastry section!

Remember that ninety percent of the real food in any grocery store is on the outer walls—the fresh produce, the meat section, and the dairy section. When you venture into the center sections you're in dangerous territory. Potato chips, packaged cookies, and little chocolate gremlin cereals will tempt you to abandon your plan, your budget, and your diet. Keep your nose buried in your shopping list. There is very little in the middle of the store that you really need. I've found that it pays for me to shop the outer walls first and then delve into the center aisles with my cart nearly full of real, nutritious foods.

While waiting your turn in the check-out line, you might find it interesting to take an informal survey of the people around you. Compare the appearance of the shoppers with the food in their shopping carts. Have you ever noticed that they match? For example, the slim, healthy-looking woman in the tennis outfit usually has a lot of fresh produce in her cart, along with yogurt, skim milk, and lean meats. The pot-bellied man chewing on a fat cigar usually pushes a cart filled with beer and pretzels. That obese woman with the pudgy children puffs along behind a shopping cart loaded down with cookies, potato chips, soda pop, sugar-coated cereals, and cartons of ice cream. In the next aisle a gentleman who has a cart full of pastries looks like the Pillsbury Dough Boy. If you eat too many doughnuts you begin to look like a doughnut—round, soft, and pale! Cart watching is one of my favorite pastimes (besides reading magazines) in the check-out line. But the only cart that really matters to me is my own, and I try to keep the foods in it worthy of putting into my family.

Once you carry your groceries out to the car, put the frozen food items in an inexpensive styrofoam cooler in your trunk. Just ask the bagger to pack all those items in the same bag. That way you don't have to rush home after you buy frozen foods. You're free to make a few more stops if you want to.

When you get home and put away the groceries, it's a good time to prepare some of your foods. Wash and dry fruits before putting them in the refrigerator. Wash vegetables well and then prepare carrot and celery sticks, along with turnip slices, for healthy dipping and snacking. Wash, dry, and tear up greens for the week's salads, storing them in a large plastic bowl with a lid. At dinner time simply put a handful of greens in each salad bowl, add whatever toppings you like, such as tomatoes, cheese, or croutons, and you have quick and easy salads. If your family, like mine, prefers the less nutritious but sweeter iceberg lettuce, you can slowly wean them onto darker green varieties by just adding a little Boston, Bibb, or Romaine lettuce in your salad greens mixture, increasing the amount over a period of time.

This is also a good time to stir up a large batch of browned ground chuck, adding salt, pepper, and onion. Place family-sized servings in plastic freezer bags so you can make quick casseroles, spaghetti, or sloppy joes later in the week. Press out hamburger patties. Divide chicken parts into separate freezer bags according to what you plan to make with them.

Throw wings and backs into a separate bag for making soup stock. By the time you finish putting away your groceries and cleaning up the kitchen, you've also done a lot of the week's food preparation.

Meal Preparation

The secret to taking the drudgery out of daily meal preparation is simple: plan ahead. The first step is having a well organized, easy-to-work-in kitchen. The second step is writing out your week's menus in advance. The third step is shopping efficiently once a week, avoiding daily time-consuming trips to the grocery store. The fourth step is washing, chopping, and cooking foods as you put away your groceries. By now 75 percent of the work is done! After all that, getting dinner onto the table every night is going to be quick work. The last step in planning for daily meal preparation is to think about what you're making for dinner tomorrow night as you clean up after dinner tonight. That's the time to take frozen meats out of the freezer and put them in the refrigerator to begin thawing. That's the time to think about when you want to begin preparing that meal tomorrow. Will it be a meal that you need to prepare at the last minute, like cubed steaks and mashed potatoes? Or will it be something that you need to start early in the day, like a casserole or soup? If so, set out the crockpot or the soup pot now so you'll see it when you go to the kitchen tomorrow morning. Have you ever realized at 5:00 p.m. that you should have started this dinner six hours ago? Setting out a reminder will help you to get an early start.

If you're making a dish that can be frozen, such as a casserole, meatloaf, or soup, why not make enough for two meals? Double the recipe and halve the work. Serve one batch that day and freeze the other to serve in a week or two. When writing out that week's menus, plan to serve your already-prepared meal on one of your busier days. You'll love yourself later.

Another helpful habit is to set the dinner table as early in the day as possible. If you have young children at home during the day, you might want to do this right after lunch. If your children are all in school, you can set the dinner table after clearing away the breakfast dishes. Finding the table already set when you begin to cook dinner relieves you of one more last-minute chore. It's especially nice to do if you're going to be out of the house all day and won't get home until late in the afternoon. And if you're running behind at dinnertime, the family will never suspect it if the table is already set!

Kim began letting her little boy Alex set the table every afternoon to keep him occupied while she prepared dinner. Today she says Alex sets the table every day without even having to be asked—and he's only four years old!

Teach family members to carefully wash their hands with warm soap and water before each meal. Most communicable diseases, such as colds and flu, are not spread primarily by airborne bacteria. One Oklahoma University study showed that we are much more likely to catch these diseases from our own dirty hands after touching doorknobs, toys, or telephones than from a sneeze or kiss.

When you serve meals, especially when the family is together in the evening, make the meal a special time. Turn off the television and turn on some relaxing background music. If you allow the children to take their turn at saying grace over the meal, they won't be afraid to pray out loud as adults. Use family mealtimes as opportunities to teach children basic table manners. What they do at the table at home is what they will do away from home—better to teach them privately than to be embarrassed publicly! Be sure to keep conversations positive, rather than allowing criticism or gossip at the table. That rule goes for adults, too.

Treat your family like guests, and they'll feel loved and will enjoy meals more. Set the table attractively, taking note of eye-catching color contrasts. Use a pretty tablecloth with a clear plastic covering to protect it from inevitable messes. Put some cut flowers from the garden in a vase or float some blossoms in a bowl of water. Serve the family in the dining room with the good china and candlelight on festive occasions like holidays or birthdays, or to celebrate an improvement on a report card. Allow the person of honor to invite a friend to share the meal with the family. This has the added value of teaching children to think of more formal dining as something very special.

These are the little extras that make a wife and mother a real homemaker and provide happy childhood memories for your children. Today not many homes are fortunate enough to have the nurturing environment that you can provide for your family by being an organized woman in the kitchen.

Action Assignments

1. Plan a Special Projects Day for reorganizing your kitchen.

2. Choose what time of the week you're going to plan your menus, clean out the refrigerator, and write your shopping list. Note it on your weekly schedule.

3. See if you can complete a week's grocery shopping without deviating from your shopping list.

4. Plan for tomorrow's dinner by thinking it through tonight.

5. Surprise your family with a special dining room dinner. Use it as an occasion to honor someone in your family.

10

Curb Appeal

Real estate agents use the term "curb appeal" to say that the outside of a house is attractive. If they drive their clients up to the curb in front of a house and the clients can't wait to go inside, they say it has curb appeal. Sometimes their clients take one look and say, "Yuk! We don't want to see that—drive on!" That house obviously lacks curb appeal.

Curb appeal is the first indicator whether the inside of the house is worth seeing. Why? Because a house that looks good on the outside usually looks good on the inside, too. I have never yet seen a house with a run down, ratty exterior that looks great on the inside. People are either neat or sloppy all over.

That's why a homemaker should care about her home's curb appeal. The exterior of your house makes a statement about your home, just as your personal appearance makes a statement about you. The statement that your house makes, however, reflects upon your entire family, not just you. Subconsciously, most people have the attitude that "quality people come from quality homes." One way to give the impression of a quality home is to see that your house has a tidy exterior rather than a sloppy one.

For the Christian homemaker, caring for the exterior appearance of her home is just one more way of being a good example for Christ. When Jesus is Lord of our lives, He is Lord of all—including the appearance of our homes. No one is going to be attracted to Christianity if Christian homemakers do not maintain a positive image in our own neighborhoods. Keeping the exterior of our homes neat, clean, and well-maintained is one way of doing just that.

Every neighborhood seems to have at least one family that doesn't seem to care about the condition of their home. The worst offenders in our neighborhood have a house that was quite attractive and valuable when it was new, but today it's the eyesore of the subdivision. It hasn't been painted in recent history; toys and junk clutter the front porch and yard; the driveway is a mass of broken, heaved, concrete chunks splattered with black grease stains; and the lawn and flower planters are pitifully neglected and weed-infested. The inside of this home is not in much better shape. This is a classic example of a home without a homemaker. And a home without a homemaker is nothing more than a hotel. So who cares about the appearance of a hotel?

But you can always tell, even by its curb appeal, when you see a home that has a real homemaker. One great example of a home that has a devoted homemaker is near my own house. This is my favorite house to look at when I stroll through the neighborhood. It's a simple, one-story house with an average-sized lot and a front-entry garage, like so many other houses in the neighborhood.

The house is well-maintained with fresh paint and clean windows. The lawn is green and well-trimmed, as are the trees and shrubs. A neat row of geraniums stands cheerily across the front of the house, and a perky potted plant hangs near the front door. Crisp curtains pull back to invite your view of a comfortable chair and sofa in one window and a pretty brass bed with a floral coverlet in the other. The total picture is one of simple homeyness and happiness. This family achieved it with nothing more than a little curb appeal in the form of well-maintained neatness.

Of course, keeping a home well-maintained can at times be expensive. But we must keep in mind that money spent on home maintenance is not a luxury—it is an investment. Maintaining the lawn and making inevitable repairs over the years can seem like an endless drain of money and energy. But remember that this money and energy will be well-spent. If you ever have to sell your home, which most Americans do on the average of every five years, all that effort will pay off. Your home will sell faster and for a higher price than it would have if you had not invested that time and money. Even if you don't plan on moving, you want to know that your property is not depreciating from neglect.

The cost of keeping a home in good condition should be an expense that you and your husband consider before buying a house, and not afterward. It's better to remain in an apartment or to purchase a condominium than it is to buy a house and then allow it to become a blight on the neighborhood. But lack of time and effort causes more neglect than lack of funds.

For example, it doesn't cost a lot to plant a few flowers and put a soft wreath on the front door. And it costs nothing at all to sweep the sidewalk and pull out weeds. But it takes a little organization to devote your time to such simple, but important, activities.

A homemaker may be the one to set the standards for the exterior appearance of her home, but she certainly shouldn't have to do all the outdoor work herself. That's why Janice talked to her husband and children about their responsibility to help with the yardwork. They decided to set Saturday mornings aside and make yardwork a family project. "My husband agreed that we can teach our children more about responsibility by doing yardwork with them than they could ever learn from us driving them from one entertaining activity to another on Saturdays."

While many of their friends are taking expensive tennis lessons, going to watch questionable movies, or spending unsupervised hours at the shopping mall, Janice's children are learning the value of getting dirty and sweaty in their own backyard. While Janice sweeps the porch and washes the windows, her husband runs the lawn mower, and her children pull weeds out of the flower beds and garden. When the weather doesn't permit outside activities, they may spend their time cleaning out the garage, the basement, or the attic. Then they get cleaned up and spend the afternoon together at the swimming pool, the park, or the library as their "reward" for getting the work done. As a result of Janice's planning, the work gets done while family ties are strengthened.

But what if you have a husband who refuses, or is unable, to help you with the outside care of your home? Then you have three choices:

1. You can pay professionals to do the work, provided you can afford it.

2. You can allow your home to deteriorate to the point of the family in my first example.

3. You can make the best of a bad situation and, along with your children, do the work yourself.

Brenda took the third choice. Her husband works many hours of overtime, including Saturdays, at his new business. Instead of insisting that he spend his one free day a week doing yardwork, Brenda and her children devote one afternoon a week to getting the yard in order so the family can spend a leisurely Sunday afternoon relaxing together. As a result, Brenda has not only avoided having an exhausted and resentful husband, but she's been an example to her son and daughter of going the extra mile without complaining.

Brenda is quite a contrast to someone I once knew whom I'll call Judy. Judy lived in a large, elegant home that could have been featured on the front cover of any interior decorating magazine. Judy had everything that any woman could desire, including a hard-working husband and two lovely daughters. Yet Judy never seemed satisfied.

Once, when giving me a tour of her immaculately decorated home, Judy took me out on their large deck overlooking private woods. When I remarked how lovely it all was, Judy only turned up her nose and said, "Just look at the condition of this yard. My husband doesn't do a thing in the yard, and you just can't hire people who care enough to do a good job."

"Then why don't you do it the way you want it?" I asked.

"Oh, you must be kidding," she replied. "I don't like to work in the yard."

How odd, I thought, that homemaking is the only career in which one can refuse to do anything one doesn't want to do just because one doesn't like to do it. I couldn't help thinking how shocked Judy would be in any other job where she would have to do some things that she didn't like to do. As a nurse, I didn't like emptying bedpans. As a real estate agent, I didn't like doing reams of paperwork with every sale. I wondered if Judy's husband liked doing everything in his job to provide her with such a luxurious lifestyle. But, nonetheless, Judy didn't do what Judy didn't like to do. Judy liked complaining instead. I often think of Judy when I catch myself complaining about my work at home.

As homemakers, the choice is up to us to set the tone for our homes, inside and out, depending on the attitude we take. It's up to us to decide whether we want to make home maintenance a source of family conflict or family togetherness. Whether we live in a mansion or a mobile home, we have the opportunity to make our homes an asset to the community and a positive witness for our faith. And it all begins with just a little curb appeal.

Here are some practical suggestions for achieving curb appeal at your home:

- Give the front entry to your home a welcoming appearance. Keep the porch and sidewalk swept clean. If there is room, make a small seating area with a porch swing or a couple of chairs. Some potted plants will soften and cheer the entryway.
- Keep the lawn well mowed and weed-free. Trim the edges of sidewalks.
- Don't be too proud to sweep up debris from the street in front of your home. Some neighbors may kid you, but others may notice your example and do the same themselves.
- Keep flower beds clean and watered. If you don't have a green thumb, you may want to fill them in with mulch and a few shrubs. It's better to have no flowers at all than to have sad, straggly ones.
- Keep shrubs neatly trimmed to avoid that aged look that overgrown, shaggy shrubs give a home. Keep shrubs in front of windows trimmed no higher than the bottom window sill. Don't allow shrubs or trees to obstruct the view of your entryway.
- Keep trees well-trimmed, especially along sidewalks. (Nothing bothers walkers more than having to duck under branches to avoid getting slapped in the face.) Lop off any branches that are growing at odd angles, and don't allow clinging vines to grow up from the base of your trees.
- Don't leave grass clippings on the street or sidewalk. (That's very tacky!) Kill grass in sidewalk cracks with chlorine bleach. Prevent new growth with a sprinkling of salt.
- Keep gutters clog-free and draining well away from the foundation of your house. (This alone would solve many people's wet basement problems.)
- Keep window treatments uniform across the front of the house. One house in our neighborhood

sports printed cafe curtains in one window, mini-blinds in another window, and draperies in yet another. That home is not nearly as attractive as a similar house with simple, white Priscillas pulled back at every window.

- Use complementary colors on the exterior of your home. Avoid overly bold, bright colors—such as the purple house in our city! On the other hand, avoid the "dull blahs" by perking up soft, neutral colors with a touch of slightly bolder contrast on trimwork.
- Keep the garage neatly organized or keep the door closed. Most people don't want anyone peeking into their messy closets, but they don't think twice about unsightly garages.
- Keep cars parked in the garage or on the driveway whenever possible to avoid cluttered, crowded streets. Encourage teenagers to confine their car repair projects to the garage.
- Teach children to pick up toys and clutter at the end of the day.

We can't all have perfect homes all the time like "Mr. Wonderful," the man in our neighborhood who never has a blade of grass out of place. But we can notice what improvements we need to make and set aside a regular time each week to give attention to those items. Slow, persistent progress pays off for those who wish to keep the outside of their homes in as good condition as the inside. That's real curb appeal.

Action Assignments

1. Plan a regular time for your outdoor work, whether it be for fifteen minutes every afternoon by yourself, or for a couple of hours every Saturday morning with the whole family.

2. Take a long walk through your neighborhood to notice the good points and bad points of each house and lawn. Determine how you can learn from others' wisdom and mistakes to improve your own home.

3. Teach your children to enjoy physical work by including them in your gardening and yardwork. Plan a family fun time as a reward for finishing the work.

Suggested Reading

Baker, Jerry. *The Impatient Gardener.* New York: Ballantine Books, 1983.

Practical how-to for do-it-yourselfers who want to keep their lawns looking good without investing a lot of money. Basic lessons in caring for trees, shrubs, and plants.

Lacy, Allen. *Home Ground: A Gardener's Miscellany.* New York: Farrar Straus Giroux, 1980, 1981, 1982, 1983, 1984.

Wonderful winter reading for cabin-bound gardeners.

11

Can Children Be Organized?

One friend with young, lively children often moans, "I'm going to get organized—just as soon as my kids are grown!" I can surely sympathize with her. I remember the days when my home seemed like Tinker Toy Land, I wished someone would manufacture wallpaper that was already decorated with little handprints, and life was measured by how many things I could get done between meals and diaper changes. While older women were wisely telling me, "Enjoy them while you can; they grow up so fast," I was wishing they would so I could get some rest!

Today, of course, I'm telling other young mothers to "enjoy them while you can," too. But I'm also telling them that you can enjoy your children more if you help them to be organized. You need to keep in mind, however, that organizing children must not be done like a staff sergeant barking orders at his troops but like a shepherd leading a flock of frisky lambs. In other words, you have to allow them room to have fun along the way.

Before teaching your children how to be organized, decide exactly what you want your child to do and why. Do you want to teach your children to be confident and to master skills that they will need as adults? Or is your motive to get the kids to do the housework so Mom can play? If so, think again!

Abdicating Responsibility?

When my children were very young and Women's Lib was in its infancy, I read a magazine article written by a woman who believed that she should not have to work at anything. She was a full-time homemaker (I use the term loosely) who only wanted to spend her time doing things she enjoyed, such as reading novels, watching TV, and shopping with friends. She had adopted the philosophy that everyone in the family should do their own laundry, cooking, and cleaning. If they didn't do it, they did without. She took care of only herself.

This article had a certain surface appeal to women who were drowning in over-busyness. But I couldn't help wondering why that woman thought she should be the only person in her family who didn't have to work. Her husband had a full-time job (or she wouldn't have had the freedom to stay home), and her children had to go to school every day. She had missed the obvious point that life is work. As Solomon said in Ecclesiastes, the only way to enjoy your life is to enjoy your work. In refusing to do for anyone but herself, this woman was teaching her children that work is bad and selfishness is good.

Today women's magazines and home organization books offer advice on how to get the rest of the family to do the housework. These publications cater to the woman who works outside the home and can't possibly do it all. The advice in these articles is usually preceded with the number one rule: "Lower your standards. Don't expect so much."

Fortunately, as full-time homemakers, we don't have to lower our standards, and we don't have to coerce our family into doing our work for us. But we should teach our kids to be neat, clean, and orderly for their own personal benefit. A mother is, more than anything else, a teacher. And lessons in how to work happily and productively will serve our children well all their lives.

How to Teach Your Kids

The first step in teaching children to be organized is to recognize what type of skills your child is capable of doing at his or her age. Expecting a three-year-old to make a bed without rumples or a five-year-old to clean a room perfectly is expecting the impossible. Be sure to gear all tasks age-appropriately.

The remaining steps are: patience, patience, patience! Kids will never get it right the first time, and they'll need endless repetition and reminders. But, since no one can learn well under pressure, kind perseverance must prevail over frustration. As one child said to his irate mother, "I can't hear you when you're screaming at me!" Children learn best when we make work into play.

To teach a child anything, one must first get him to concentrate on the task at hand. My Uncle Mitch, an avid coon hunter, knows this truth has a much broader application. Because his rotund stature prevents him from being able to navigate the rugged Oklahoma terrain, he rides mules, which he has taught to leap over creeks and fences. A local newspaper interviewed my Uncle Mitch and asked him, "How on earth do you teach stubborn mules to jump over fences?"

"Well," Uncle Mitch answered sagely, "the first step is to get their attention!"

That's also the first step in teaching children.

When Chris teaches her preschooler any new task, she first sits down and talks to him about it.

"Matt, today Mommy is going to teach you how to put away the toys after playing outside. We must always put our toys away because we don't want them to get lost or rained on. So I will show you how I want you to put away your toys before coming back in the house."

Then Chris shows Matt how to bring the toys into the garage and put them in the correct place.

"Look, Matt. This is your toy box, and this is where you can park your Big Wheel. Let me show you how to put your toys away, and then you can try it."

Always demonstrate a task before asking the child to do it, no matter how simple it seems to you. Encourage him to repeat the instructions back to you and to ask questions about anything he doesn't understand. Never belittle a child's efforts, no matter how clumsy or imperfect they may be. Gently correct him and be sure to praise him for his efforts.

"That's wonderful, Matt," Chris says, "I like the way you brought your toys into the garage. But remember to put them in this box. Why don't you try it again, honey?"

With encouragement Matt puts away his toys without being reminded. But as soon as Chris forgets to praise him, Matt forgets to put away his toys. Rather than scolding him, Chris says, "Matt, remember to put away your toys. Let's go outside so Mommy can see how well you do that!"

When teaching a child to keep his room neat and orderly, give him furniture and storage boxes that are scaled down to his size. Tiny hands have a hard time manipulating big items. Imagine how overwhelmed you would feel if your kitchen counters were above your head and all the pots and utensils were twice their normal size. It would probably discourage you from cooking dinner!

When our older son Scot was born, he was the first grandchild on both sides of the family. Of course, nothing was too good for this grandchild, and soon he was surrounded with the biggest and best of everything. He had the biggest red wagon, the biggest toybox, and the biggest rocking horse in our apartment complex. But he was such a little boy! His favorite toys were little wooden blocks and tiny plastic toy soldiers. They were just his size!

When teaching children to put away toys and clothing, remember to keep shelves and clothing rods low and easily accessible to your child's height. Provide them with plenty of colorful plastic crates for keeping all sorts of treasures and collectibles. Give them a place to keep artwork, marbles, rocks, and bottle caps. Most children are happy to help Mommy decide which special pictures she should store in their "memory box" and which ones she should discard to make space for new things. You may want to keep a cardboard box in the basement or attic for permanent storage of such memorabilia.

If your child needs help in remembering what items belong in what place, you can tape pictures of specific items in the bottom of the container or tack a photo on the back of the shelf where he should store them. This makes it more fun for the child, like matching puzzle pieces. If he needs help remembering his grooming tasks, you can also take photos of your child brushing his teeth, combing his hair, putting away his pajamas, and making his bed. Paste them onto a poster to remind him what to do each morning.

Older children can benefit from work charts with daily chores written under each day of the week. After discussing the need for organization in assigning and remembering daily tasks, your family can plan together who should do what chores, make up a chart, and post it on the refrigerator or bulletin board. Praise should be a child's daily reward for a job well done, rather than money or bribes. And punishment for not doing assigned work should be decided upon beforehand as a family. Perhaps forgetfulness will carry the penalty of an apology and doing an extra task, or helping a brother or sister do one of their jobs.

What About Discipline?

Because children forget things out of their immaturity, spankings shouldn't be used to punish childish forgetfulness.

Spankings can make learning and working a thing to be dreaded, rather than an enjoyable growing process.

Paula, a homemaker with a lot of experience in teaching children, once told me, "We only give our children spankings for three things: disobedience, dishonesty, and disrespect. Disobedience does not mean forgetfulness, but rather means willful refusal to obey us. Dishonesty is any untruth, no matter how small. Disrespect is any word or action that shows rebellion against our authority as their parents." Paula's children are among the best behaved and happiest that I have seen.

As children grow older and more mature, spankings should become less and less frequent. If not, there may be too much rigidness or too little consistency by the parents. We've all seen cases of both just visiting the grocery store! When children reach school age and are old enough to remember their indiscretions without immediate action, it's a good time to transfer the spanking responsibilities to your husband. Physical punishment becomes more emotionally stressful for a mother and her child as the child grows older. I can tell you from experience that it's impossible to spank a child who towers over you!

My husband Mark once told me, "When I grew up, Dad was the disciplinarian and Mom was the one who nurtured. If I did something wrong, I knew Mom would tell Dad. He would give me a good talking to or a spanking. It made me respect both of them." Once our children were past the baby stage, I was as eager to turn that job over to him as he was to take it.

Todd, our younger son, got his last spanking when he was in the fourth grade. He did something at school that merited a visit with the principal from my husband and me. When we got home, Mark took Todd to the privacy of our bedroom, closed the door, and explained that his actions deserved punishment. At this point Todd still had an angry and rebellious attitude.

Mark then administered a hard spanking until our son broke and the tears began to fall. Then Mark held Todd tightly in his arms, hugging him and telling him how much he loved him. It was a very emotional experience, and one that I could never have carried off quite so well. When Mark and Todd emerged from that room, there was a new closeness between them. A little boy who could have gone down the wrong road has grown up to be an honor student at the United States Air Force Academy.

Sow Good Seed

The Bible conveys a spiritual truth that applies to every parent. "Do not be deceived, God is not mocked; for whatever a man sows, this he will also reap" (Galatians 6:7). Most of us who are able to choose a stay-at-home career do so primarily for the sake of raising and nurturing our children properly. We want to be sure that the seed sown in our children will be good seed. We don't wish to entrust that important seed planting to strangers at daycare centers. Our teaching and example insures that the seed we plant in our tender, young children will last a lifetime. Seed will inevitably sprout and bear fruit, whether for good or for evil. This involves every area of your child's life—manners, organization, and his morality.

God's Word emphasizes the responsibility to sow good seed in our children and to consider children a blessing from Him. This cuts against the grain of the current theory that children are influenced ninety percent by genetics and environment and only ten percent by parental influence. And it directly opposes society's attitude that children are more a burden than a blessing.

For that reason, we must be mindful of the seed we sow in our children's lives. We must remember that seeds of home-centeredness are sown by encouraging home-centered activities. We must also remember that seeds of rebellion and evil are sown by exposing a child to literature, television, movies, music, or people with ungodly values. What a child sees, he will emulate.

For that reason many parents have chosen to prohibit anything from their homes that does not honor God. They prohibit any literature, television, movies, or toys that glorify violence. They refuse to allow their children to make idols of rock stars who promote drugs, violence, and rebellion. They also ban attitudes of materialism, snobbishness, and prejudice from their homes. They do this in obedience to God's Word, which says, "Neither shalt thou bring an abomination into thine house, lest thou be a cursed thing like it" (Deuteronomy 7:26, KJV). Many young people today have, indeed, become "a cursed thing," like the ungodly things their parents permit them to bring into their homes.

When our sons were in elementary school, they wanted to start a beer can collection like their friends were doing. I said no to that, telling them that they could collect soda cans instead. A short time later they wanted to know if they could buy a record album by the rock group "K.I.S.S." (which allegedly stands for Knights In Satan's Service.) I firmly told them that under no conditions were they ever to bring into our home any record or poster with evil-looking people on it. As they grew older we had to establish firm limits on movies we permitted them to see, all in spite of what their friends were doing.

Liberal psychology tells us that this is censorship and that we should allow our children to grow up without the influence of our values so that they can "decide for themselves" when they are older. God's Word tells us that it's our responsibility as parents to protect our children from evil, and to "train up a child in the way he should go, even when he is old he will not depart from it" (Proverbs 22:6).

We eventually moved out of that neighborhood, but a few years later we learned that our children's playmates who did all those "normal things that kids do today" had become involved with drugs and immorality. Their homes had become unhappy war zones instead of places of refuge from the world. We thanked God for giving us the courage to ban such unhealthy influences from our home from the very beginning.

In his book *Set the Trumpet to Thy Mouth,* David Wilkerson wrote, "There is enough hell for them [our children] to face outside the home. The home should be a holy, sanctified sanctuary, a place of rest and peace from the corruption of the age—and a place where Jesus is real and the Holy Spirit ever present."[1]

Of course, the strongest influence in our children's lives is that of our own personal example. That's why it's important for us as homemakers to present an example of cleanliness, orderliness, and godliness in all aspects of our lives. There are no guarantees that our children will turn out exactly as we wish they would, no matter how "perfect" we may try to be as their parents. But we are obliged to do our best with the children God has given us for as long as we have them. The rest is up to God, and to our children themselves.

Recently our family attended the college graduation of Scot, our older son. One of Scot's neighbors, who liked and befriended him during his years at college, attended the ceremony with our family. She repeatedly said to us, "You must have done something right when you raised that boy!" Finally I replied, "Well, I guess we will take the liberty of accepting your compliment. But if Scot had turned out badly, it would have been all his fault!"

Not all of us were born natural "earth mothers" who knew instinctively how to do everything right—certainly not me! But as we mature in Christ, He leads us through every difficulty and mistake for His name's sake. Even in child-rearing it is true: "There is therefore now no condemnation for those who are in Christ Jesus" (Romans 8:1). That's a good scripture to remember at the end of a frustrating day.

To teach a child discipline and organization, we must be very consistent in enforcing our rules. One teacher told me, "Consistency and discipline walk hand in hand. You can't have one without the other. If you make a rule, you must always follow through on it. If you decide it was a bad rule, explain to the child why you are changing your mind so he won't be confused." If we considered all the effort it takes to enforce every rule, we would probably be more prudent about the rules we make.

The following is a list of household rules published by Christian Life Workshops,[2] and I can't think of a better set of instructions to live by:

The Rules of This House

1. We obey our Lord Jesus Christ.
2. We love and honor one another.
3. We tell the truth.
4. We consider one another's interests ahead of our own.
5. We speak quietly and respectfully with one another.
6. We do not hurt one another with unkind words or deeds.
7. When someone needs correction, we correct him in love.
8. When someone is sorry, we forgive him.
9. When someone is sad, we comfort him.
10. When someone is happy, we rejoice with him.
11. When we have something nice to share, we share it.
12. When we have work to do, we do it without complaining.
13. We take good care of everything God has given us.

14. We do not create unnecessary work for others.
15. When we open something, we close it.
16. When we turn something on, we turn it off.
17. When we take something out, we put it away.
18. When we make a mess, we clean it up.
19. When we do not know what to do, we ask.
20. When we go out, we act just as if we were in this house.
21. When we disobey or forget any of the Rules of This House, we accept the discipline and instruction of the Lord.

The most important reason we strive to teach our children to be organized is not to have an immaculate house, but rather to help develop their character. Just as the military requires cleanliness and organization to develop discipline for more important duties, we teach our children to be organized about little things in the hope that one day they will be equipped to be responsible in much larger matters.

One day, when your children are grown and gone, you'll have time for a perfect house. What matters now is not the house, but the home; and not the children's duties, but the children. To every mother of young children who worries herself unnecessarily with trying to do too much, I can only say, "There is an appointed time for everything. And there is a time for every event under heaven" (Ecclesiastes 3:1).

If you're feeling overburdened by your responsibilities to church, school, and community, take heart. You can fulfill your duties as a good citizen when your kids are grown and in college. The most noble task you can do for God, for your community, and for your country is to raise good citizens today. If that's all you accomplish in your lifetime, you will have accomplished more than most famous people! Take it from one who knows, and "Enjoy them while you can!"

Action Assignments

1. Evaluate what age-appropriate duties you want to teach to your children.

2. Call a family conference and discuss why you wish to teach responsibilities to your children. Have them help you in suggesting what duties they should assume. Decide in advance what punishment will be incurred for failure to complete each duty.

3. Post a "Duty Sheet" for older children. Take photos and make a poster of "Things To Do" for younger children.

4. Heap on the praise and encouragement for positive efforts.

5. Post "The Rules of This House" for a permanent reminder to everyone of expected behavior.

Suggested Reading

Horton, Marilee. *Free to Stay at Home*. Waco, TX: Word Books, 1982.

Pride, Mary. *The Way Home: Beyond Feminism, Back to Reality*. Westchester, IL: Crossway Books, 1985.

——*All the Way Home: Power for Your Family to Be its Best*. Westchester, IL: Crossway Books, 1989.

12

How to Handle a Husband

In the musical *Camelot*, King Arthur asks a wise little wizard named Merlin the age-old question, "How do you handle a woman?" Many homemakers today wish they had Merlin around to give them the magical answer to "How do you handle a husband?"

"My husband is such a sloppy person! All I ever do is clean up after him," is a frequent complaint from wives who are tired of picking up a trail of shoes, neckties, and underwear from the floor.

"My husband is a sports addict," complain many others. "He sits glued to every football, baseball, and basketball game on television. As soon as one season is over, the other has already begun. How can I ever get him to pay attention to me or help out around the house?"

Another wife groans, "My husband is a workaholic. He spends more time at the office than he does at home. The children are beginning to wonder who he is!"

Husband problems are innumerable. Fortunately, however, we don't have to rely on a fictitious magician for our answers. We have a much better marriage guide, which was written by the One who created marriage in the first place.

Following God's Order

In the book of Genesis we find Adam in the Garden of Eden (a perfect place, even neater than Hawaii) naming all the animals, dining on luscious fruits, and best of all, never having to clock in at the office. Don't you think Adam would have been perfectly happy in such a Utopian existence? But no! Even his Creator said, "It is not good for the man to be alone. I will make him a helper suitable for him" (Genesis 2:18).

So God created Eve for Adam, and woman for man. Too often we have the wrong impression that man was created to be a helpmeet to woman! Ever since that day there have been problems between the sexes. (Remember the apple?)

Fortunately, however, God gave us the rest of the Bible, which is filled with Holy Spirit inspired ideas for getting along together. These ideas worked well until this generation. That's when so-called "Women's Liberation" came into vogue and discarded God's plan for marriage. As a result, today one out of every two marriages ends in divorce. But the divorce rate is only one out of every forty marriages for those who attend church together. And for those couples who attend church, read their Bibles, and pray together, only one out of every 142 marriages end in divorce! So it might behoove us to re-examine God's plan for "how to handle a husband."

We could boil the Scriptures down to this simple formula: "Wives, treat your husbands as reverently and respectfully as you would treat the Lord Jesus Christ. Have a submissive, rather than a defiant, attitude. Let your beauty be more than just a lovely appearance, but rather an inward gentleness and quietness of spirit, which is precious to God" (paraphrased from 1 Peter 3:1-6; Ephesians 5:22-33).

Regarding our role at home, Titus 2:3-5 tells us, "Older women likewise are to be reverent in their behavior, not malicious gossips, nor enslaved to much wine, teaching what is good, that they may encourage the young women to love their husbands, to love their children, to be sensible, pure, workers at home, kind, being subject to their own husbands, that the word of God may not be dishonored."

Did you ever stop to think that disobedience to any of those commands causes the Word of God to be dishonored? But many Christian women balk at being under the protective headship of their husbands because they don't like the big no-no word "submit"! It rubs us the wrong way, especially in our culture of individuality and independence.

But, interpreted correctly, submission is not a word that means "slavery," but rather "servant." A slave is a person who serves because she has to. A servant is one who serves because she chooses to. Submission is also a way of letting God deal with your husband instead of having your husband fight against you. If you tell your husband that you disagree with him on a particular decision, and then argue and sulk, your actions may cause him to feel defensive and justified in his stance. But if you explain your point of view and then defer to his decision in the end, letting him know you are trusting God to guide him—that puts him on the spot! As one pastor succinctly put it, "Submission is ducking so God can hit your husband."

Scripture gives us good examples of wives who practiced God's successful principles. Some of my favorites are Priscilla, who faithfully helped her husband with their tentmaking business and functioned as his teammate in ministering the gospel to others (see Acts 18:26), and Sarah, who Scripture tells us, "obeyed Abraham, calling him Lord." The Bible also says, "and you have become her children if you do what is right without being frightened by any fear" (1 Peter 3:6). As long as you're submitting to your husband "as is fitting in the Lord" (meaning not in any sinful thing), you need not be afraid of the results. (See Colossians 3:18.)

But my favorite wife is the godly woman in Proverbs 31, of whom it is said, "The heart of her husband trusts in her, and he will have no lack of gain. She does him good and not evil all the days of her life" (Proverbs 31:11,12). As a result of her faithfulness, her husband praises her, saying, "Many daughters have done nobly, but you excel them all!" (Proverbs 31:29).

What Every Husband Craves

All the successful wives in God's Word gave their husband something that every husband covets more than money, fame, or even sex! Most husbands are starving for it. And it's something that guarantees a happy husband. What is this secret ingredient? It's spelled R-E-S-P-E-C-T.

The Bible says, "Let each individual among you also love his own wife even as himself; and let the wife see to it that she respect her husband" (Ephesians 5:33). Why doesn't the Bible say, "and let the wife see to it that she love her husband," too? I believe that's because the best way we can love our husbands is to treat them with respect. Any husband not receiving respect can never feel loved.

Respect means never belittling, nagging, or being rude. Respect implies courtesy, kindness, and admiration. Respect is not making your husband drive a car with a personalized license plate that reads "DUM-DUM," like one I saw a man driving! And it's not putting a bumper sticker on your car that says, "Husband and Dog Lost: Reward for Dog." They're funny, but how would they make your husband feel? Godly humor never sacrifices someone else's respect. Every husband should be treated with respect, if for no other reason than for the position he holds as a husband. A man is more motivated to behave in a manner deserving respect if his wife treats him respectfully.

I've also learned that respect includes nurturing. If you think you need to nurture only your children, think again! Husbands hide tender, little-boy hearts deep inside and will soak up nurturing like thirsty flowers soak up the gentle rain.

If you don't believe it, just try giving your husband a few hugs, kisses, and sweet words tonight. Bring him a little snack, treat him like a guest in his own home, and talk to him as tenderly as you would to a young child—and watch him bloom!

An Ungodly Woman's Influence

Besides many good examples, the Bible also records the example of an ungodly woman who did everything opposed to God's plan for a wife. Her name was Jezebel. She led her husband Ahab, the king of Israel, into Baal worship. Baal worshipers disgusted God because they killed their children as sacrifices. God states that He will bring calamity upon those who worship Baal "because they have forsaken Me and have . . . filled this place with the blood of the innocent and have built the high places of Baal to burn their sons in the fire as burnt offerings to Baal, a thing which I never commanded or spoke of, nor did it ever enter My mind" (Jeremiah 19:4,5).

Jezebel had several other bad qualities, too. She was a murderess, a manipulator, and an enemy of God's servants. The Bible says, "Surely there was no one like Ahab who sold himself to do evil in the sight of the Lord, because Jezebel his wife incited him" (1 Kings 21:25). Her life is a chilling example of the power that a woman can have over her husband for evil.

Sadly, today many women have become infected by the same spirit that drove Jezebel. Rather than walking in obedience to God's Word, they choose to embrace the values and attitudes of the world. They care more about what they think is right than what God says is right. In short, they are women who choose to have a Jezebel spirit rather than the spirit of the godly wife in Proverbs 31.

Here's a list of some qualities of a Jezebel spirit versus a godly spirit:

Comparison of

Today's Jezebel Spirit:	Today's Godly Spirit:
Idol worship (Women's rights, materialism, etc.)	Worships God in "spirit and in truth" (John 4:24).
Sacrifices children (abortion, neglect, abuse)	Loves children (Titus 2:4) and considers them gifts from God.
Lords over her husband. Manipulates to have her own way.	Is subject to her husband and defers to him. (Ephesians 5:22)
Loves things of the world.	Loves things of God.
Has worldly values.	Has scriptural values.
Is loud, overly talkative, draws attention to herself.	Has a quiet spirit. Draws attention to Jesus Christ. (1 Peter 3:4)
Dresses in an unfeminine, seductive, or ostentatious manner.	Dresses in a chaste, feminine manner. (1 Peter 3:2,3)
Is not content to work at home.	Is a "worker at home" (Titus 2:5). (Not a loafer at home.)
Speaks evil of her husband. Holds a grudge against him.	Does her husband "good and not evil all the days of her life" (Proverbs 31:12).
Keeps secrets from her husband or deceives him.	"The heart of her husband trusts in her" (Proverbs 31:11).
Has others serve her.	Nurtures and serves others.

Is lazy and hates housework.	"Looks well to the ways of her household, and does not eat the bread of idleness" (Proverbs 31:13).
Complains, makes excuses, and procrastinates.	"Works with her hands in delight" (Proverbs 31:27).
Gossips, meddles in other people's business, is rude, tactless, and opinionated. (1 Timothy 5:13)	Tactful, doesn't offer advice unless she is asked, does not talk unless she has something worthwhile to say. (Titus 2:3)
Talks constantly about herself and her problems. "I, me, mine," etc.	Seldom refers to herself or her problems in conversation.

The list could go on and on, but these are a few examples of behavior to avoid and to emulate.

God's Mandate for Husbands

"So what about my husband?" you ask. "What does Scripture say he should do?"

Here's a simple scriptural formula for husbands: "Husbands, love your wives just as sacrificially as Christ loved the church. Protect and care for her, sheltering her from the cares of the world. Treat her as you would treat your own body, for you are now one flesh. Prefer her above all others" (paraphrased from Ephesians 5:25-32).

Regarding a husband's role in the home, Scripture bluntly states, "But if anyone does not provide for his own, and especially for those of his household, he has denied the faith, and is worse than an unbeliever" (1 Timothy 5:8).

This obviously puts the financial burden on the husband, leaving his wife free to manage the home and nurture the children. It also implies that the wife should not put unnecessary, frivolous financial demands on her husband so that he can fulfill his obligation in this area. In this day of inflation and high taxes, husband and wife must work as a team if they want to keep the wife in the home—and it is work! He works hard to bring the money home, and she works hard to make it stretch as far as possible by being industrious and frugal.

Obviously, it helps the husband fulfill his scriptural roles if the wife fulfills hers, and visa-versa. A man is not motivated to work hard and be loving for a sloppy, complaining, selfish woman. And it's very difficult for a woman to have a sweet, submissive attitude toward a man who is hateful and controlling! This is often the problem when one partner is a Christian and the other is not. (I suggest my book, *How to be the Happy Wife of an Unsaved Husband* to those in that predicament.)

Motivating Your Spouse

If you're having problems with your husband—and who doesn't from time to time?—the best way to motivate him to act the way you want him to is for you to act the way he wants you to. The Golden Rule, "Do unto others as you would have them do unto you," really does bring results!

Is your husband driving you to distraction by throwing his dirty clothes on the floor and leaving a trail of clutter behind him? First, try to politely (as opposed to accusingly) let him know that you would appreciate his thoughtfulness in this area. Gentle reminders, rather than nagging, help.

Second, provide your husband with easy access to a clothes hamper, and let him know where things belong. (Sometimes husbands don't realize that. This helped my husband immensely, much to my surprise.)

Finally, if all else fails, see if you can pick up after him without complaining (to yourself or to others) as an offering of thankfulness to the Lord for providing you with your husband. I read a touching anecdote in *Reader's Digest* about a woman who was visiting a friend. As they sat talking in the kitchen, the friend's husband tracked mud across her spotless floor. The visitor remarked to the wife, "His boots certainly do bring the dirt in." "Yes," the smiling wife replied as she got up to get the broom. "But they bring him in, too." This couple had been married for fifty-four years, and you can see why.

Does your husband sit for hours on end in front of the television, watching sports or John Wayne movies? Once again, you might try telling him how you feel about this. See if you can compromise so that he watches less TV and you spend more time doing other things with him. Make sure he's not watching television to escape from you or from problems he can't deal with.

See if you can encourage him to find other means of relaxation. If all else fails, just consider the time your husband spends in front of the television to be free time for you, too. Find a hobby you can enjoy while he's being a couch potato.

But be sure you don't begrudge your husband a fair amount of time doing whatever he enjoys, whether it is watching TV, golfing, fishing, or any other non-harmful activity. One woman I know complains bitterly about the few weekends her husband spends away on hunting trips. "I need him here to help me with the kids. I'm with them all the time, and he should help me with them when he isn't at work," she says. This woman forgets that she doesn't have to contend with his job and his boss every day. Husbands need some time off, too. Men need time alone and time spent with friends as much as women do. A relaxed, happy husband is a lot easier to live with than one who isn't!

If you can't draw your husband's attention away from his hobby, try something novel—join him! I know one wife who enjoys duck hunting and another who thinks it's great fun to stalk deer. When my husband bought a hot-air balloon, I took pilot's lessons with him—not because I wanted the responsibility of flying, but because I wanted to share a new interest with him.

Another way to get your husband to pay attention to you is to be available. Use the hours your husband is at work to do your housework. Then use the hours he is home to be with him, rather than to do the ironing or paint the bathroom. As we saw in Chapter 2, housework requires fewer hours if we're properly organized. Making your evening hours family time can have a major impact on family togetherness.

I know of one woman who complains to anyone who will listen about her husband and her marriage. But it's no wonder they enjoy no partnership. She attends the following activities alone: Sunday, church; Monday evening, aerobics class; Tuesday evening, church evangelism visits; Wednesday evening, church again; and Thursday evening, Bible study. That leaves two days a week in which to try to build a relationship with her husband. I believe the devil would rather see us spending all our time in church or anywhere else if it will keep us from spending time with our husband and children!

Being an on-the-go wife and mother can add a lot of stress to your family, but the workaholic husband can be a difficult problem, too. This man is compulsively obsessed with his career and "getting ahead" to the point of neglecting his family. He leaves his wife alone to deal with all the weighty decisions at home and provides very little role-modeling for the children.

If you're unable to communicate your needs as a wife and mother in having more time with your husband, you might try Christian counseling or a couple's retreat. He needs to understand that providing financially for his family is not his sole responsibility as a husband and father. He needs to learn scriptures that show his responsibility to teach and discipline his children, as well as to love and cherish his wife. Your husband needs to learn to relax and enjoy life himself.

Put it in Perspective

If your husband is a workaholic, avoid the temptation to argue and complain. Provide a home environment that is pleasant in the hope that your husband will be enticed to spend more time there. But if he proves to be an incorrigible workaholic, accept the good (he is providing well for you) and spend your time alone constructively. Rather than seeking solace in soap operas or destructive affairs, turn your loss to gain by spending your extra time managing your home well or doing volunteer work for the needy. (Nothing takes your mind off your problems like helping those with worse ones.)

I once read, "We cannot make people over. Our business is to make ourselves better and others happy, and that is enough to keep us busy." How true. There is also a wise Jamaican proverb that says, "Before you marry, keep both eyes open; after you marry, shut one."

It may not always be easy to be married to your husband, but few worthwhile things in life are ever easy. The alternative, divorce, is certainly not easy, either. Especially when you consider that over half of divorced husbands fail to financially support, or even to see, their children.

"The divorce epidemic not only has devastated childhood, it has brought financial ruin to millions of women," stated a White House report on the American family. "Divorce reform was supposed to be a panacea for women trapped in bad marriages. It has trapped many of them in poverty."

Facing problems like that should put picking up a pair of dirty socks in proper perspective! To maintain a happy marriage, we must avoid the temptation to make mountains out of molehills. We can do that best by not complaining about things that don't really matter. One British saying goes, "Faults are thick where love is thin."

That brings us back to old Merlin, who gave his sage advise to King Arthur in *Camelot*. If it were revised for the female gender it would go: "How to handle a husband? Listen well, and I'll tell you, dear. The way to handle a husband is to love him. Simply love him. Merely love him, love him, love him!"

Now, isn't that just what Jesus would say?

Action Assignments

1. Read the Scriptures regarding marriage. Pray for God's guidance on how you can improve your marriage through applying His Word to your specific situation.

2. Think of ways for providing more enjoyable "together" activities with your husband. Arrange your schedule so that your evenings can be spent with your husband and children, rather than doing housework.

3. Practice nurturing your husband. Find ways that you can minister love, caring, and tenderness to the secret, little-boy heart hidden within him.

Suggested Reading

Davis, Linda. *How to be the Happy Wife of an Unsaved Husband.* Springdale, PA: Whitaker House, 1986.

I wrote this for the unequally-yoked wife after my husband became a Christian—after 15 years of marriage.

Dillow, Linda. *Creative Counterpart.* Nashville, TN: Thomas Nelson Publishers, 1986.

More in-depth study of the marriage relationship for the Christian wife, with Bible study outline.

13
Time for Yourself

Julie is a wonderful wife and mother, always there when her family needs her. She entertains her husband's business clients. She's a Girl Scout leader. She teaches Sunday school. Julie even manages to keep organized with all this activity. Her home is neat and clean, and her family can depend on a delicious meal at the end of each day. Julie's family and friends adore her. To everyone who knows her, Julie is a smashing success. She is Superwoman!

But Julie does have one problem. She isn't happy! In fact, she often suffers from depression and migraines. She can't imagine why other people admire her when she feels so unfulfilled herself. And Julie has no idea what to do about it.

Today many "successful" homemakers suffer from Julie's problem. They are smiling on the outside but crying on the inside, and often no one has the slightest clue why. They think that they should be happy, but they know they aren't. And they don't know why!

If Julie was your friend and asked you for advice, what would you tell her? Would you tell her to visit a psychiatrist? (Are you aware of the high suicide rate among psychiatrists?) Would you tell her to go on a shopping spree? (Is she rich?)

Would you tell her she needs to find fulfillment in a new career? (Have you ever heard of jumping out of the frying pan into the fire?)

Or would you tell Julie, "For heaven's sake, girl, take some time out for yourself!" If so, I would heartily agree. In the elusive pursuit of perfection, we often forget all about the ones we are trying to perfect—ourselves! What good would it do if we somehow achieved perfection only to find nothing left of ourselves to enjoy it?

Alexandra Stoddard, author and interior designer, says, "Take ten percent of every single day to spend on yourself. If you can't take ten percent today, take twenty percent tomorrow. You can accrue the time over a week, but you must take it in a week. It is essential."

"But I don't have time," we often object. "I have too much work to do!" And yet, how much work will we get done if we're sick, tired, and worn to a frazzle? We must find time for ourselves—and if not for ourselves, for the family that depends upon us. Just as a car runs out of gas, we will come to a halt without the necessary fuel. Taking time for our own needs is like refueling the car. It may be an interruption in the day, but it must be done to get anywhere.

Every wife and mother has needs on three levels. She owes it to herself and her family to care for the following needs daily.

1. Physical needs
2. Mental/emotional needs
3. Spiritual needs

Let's discuss creative ways to care for ourselves in each of these areas.

Level One: Physical Needs

In previous generations some misguided Christians took the attitude that the body is an evil, temporal thing and

therefore of no value. They considered physic;
be a sin! Fortunately, today most of us consic
to be a gift from God. (Why else would He |
resurrected one when Christ returns?) God wants us to enjoy
our body without letting it rule us, so we should seriously
consider His command to take proper care of it.

> Or do you not know that your body is a temple
> of the Holy Spirit who is in you, whom you have
> from God, and that you are not your own? For you
> have been bought with a price: therefore glorify
> God in your body—1 Corinthians 6:19,20.

When God dwelt in an earthly temple, the people brought
the firstfruits of their harvests to offer them as sacrifices to
the Lord. Imagine them bringing heaping baskets of golden
grain, their shiniest fresh fruits and vegetables, and their
healthiest animals as an offering to God in His temple.

Ever since the day of Pentecost, God has chosen to dwell
in us, His children, in the form of the Holy Spirit. So every
time you set food before yourself, you're actually present-
ing an offering to God's temple! That means we must consider whether our meals and snacks are fit offerings. Am
I offering the freshest fruits and vegetables and the healthiest meats? Or am I offering God's temple potato chips, diet
colas, and corn curls?

You Are What You Eat

Everything we eat needs to be not only acceptable to our
taste buds, but an acceptable offering to the Holy Spirit in
us—not because the Holy Spirit is picky, but because He
cares about us. He knows that whatever we eat becomes part
of us, and changes us for better or for worse. Have you ever
heard the saying, "You are what you eat"? It's true. The body
of a person who eats too many pastries eventually becomes

soft and pasty-looking—and sickly. But the body of a person whose diet consists of mostly fresh fruits and vegetables will look as firm and trim as a cucumber—and be just as healthy and alive. We can be of much more service to God and to others if we are healthy and energetic.

What's the first step in caring for your body? *Eat only those foods that will create a healthy, energetic body.* It helps if you don't put anything in your mouth before offering it up to the Lord in prayer—that really makes you think about whether you ought to eat it!

Concentrate on filling each meal with natural, God-made foods, as fresh from the farm as possible. Instead of making fatty meats and white breads the core of the meal, make heaping bowls of fresh vegetables and whole grain breads the largest part of your meals. Use meats as flavorings or side dishes. The other day I made a big pot of fresh string beans, zucchini, and onions, flavored with a bit of ham. After eating two generous portions, my husband smiled and said, "That was better than dessert!"

During the day, sip real fruit juices (read the label to avoid sugary substitutes), or simply sip a glass of ice water with a wedge of lemon. You'll get to the point that you can't stand the taste of fizzing, chemical soda pop! Make yourself eat at least two pieces of fresh fruit daily—you won't believe the improvement in your complexion, energy, and regularity. If you think these foods are too expensive, consider the money you'll save by not buying junk food and by not visiting the doctor so often. A high-fiber, low-fat diet is a terrific savings, both to your body and to your pocketbook.

Burning Calories at Home

Step two of caring for your physical needs is *exercise!* Yes, girls, moving that body around is important, even though it just wants to sit. Our pastor once said, "If you give your body its way, it will kill you!" He's right. The body is just made of flesh—and the flesh must be mortified. But that need not mean purchasing a thousand dollar membership at Cher's favorite workout spa to "bust your buns"!

Years ago, when my mother-in-law moved to a new neighborhood, she said to me, "Can you imagine what the lady next door does? She pays someone to clean her house. And then she pays to exercise at the health club. Now isn't that silly? She could get her exercise by cleaning her own house, and it wouldn't cost her a cent!"

Did you know that you can burn off just as many calories by doing housework as you can by working out on Nautilus equipment? You can expend just as much energy behind a vacuum sweeper as you can behind a stationary bicycle—and have something constructive to show for it. Who says that lifting weights makes your biceps any better than scrubbing the bathtub or lifting the baby? One recent book states, "What's got four walls, a yard, and the potential for offering more forms of exercise than any fitness device ever designed? Yes, the average home. Between the sweeping, scraping, painting, polishing, shoveling, hammering and weeding, there's not a muscle of the body untouched."[1]

But for cardiovascular conditioning we need aerobic exercise to raise the heart rate and improve the circulation. Find an aerobic activity that you enjoy, and you'll actually look forward to exercising. You might try bicycling. You don't have to invest in a lot of gear to pedal the old Schwinn around the neighborhood and enjoy the sights. Or you might try tennis or swimming, which you can enjoy inside at the local YMCA or high school gym. Of course, anyone with health problems should set up a doctor-supervised exercise program. Everyone should schedule an annual check-up.

My exercise of choice is brisk walking. It doesn't stress the joints like jogging does. It doesn't require anything but a good pair of walking shoes and some old, loose-fitting clothes. I can do it any time of the day. It's free. You can even walk the dog, push the baby carriage, talk with a friend, or talk to God while doing it. What more could you want? In good weather I walk in the neighborhood, but during bad weather I walk inside at the local shopping mall.

The benefits of exercising at least three times a week for half an hour or more are tremendous. Physical activity releases brain chemicals that help to eliminate emotional depression. Increased circulation strengthens the heart, helps your muscles to assume their proper position and tone, helps your organs to function more smoothly, and even improves mental function and memory. I also find that exercise helps me to get a much better night's sleep.

It's OK to Nap

And that brings up step three in your body-care program: *Get plenty of rest.* Recent trends advise us to get by on as little sleep as possible. I've read articles encouraging people to sleep as little as five hours a night to make more time for achieving success during the day.

But no matter how much I try to get by on little sleep, my body keeps score and eventually demands repayment. I've learned that I just need a good night's rest. My performance lags if I try to get by on less. If I hit a tired afternoon slump, I have no qualms whatsoever about grabbing a nap. I wake up refreshed and ready to go full speed again—and usually accomplish much more than if I had pushed myself until bedtime.

In her book, *First We Have Coffee,*[2] author Margaret Jensen tells how her mother raised a houseful of children with much faith, frugality, and ingenuity. Yet as industrious as she was, every afternoon she had her nap. She needed it to bridge the busy hours from early morning to late evening. Small children not withstanding, she took that nap!

A neurologist at the University of Ottawa stated, "People are biologically wired for one nap a day, typically in mid-afternoon." He also said, "People whose jobs require a high level of vigilance . . . should be allowed to take scheduled naps. It may be the best way to improve their alertness, productivity, and overall performance.''³ Can you think of anyone whose job requires more vigilance than a mother?

Recent research by the Sleep Disorders and Research Center of Detroit's Henry Ford Hospital confirms our need for rest. They proved with test subjects that increasing sleeping time by two hours a night (from seven up to nine hours of sleep per night) resulted in increased work performance scores. According to the research director, "People appear to benefit from getting as much sleep as they can.''⁴

When talking about physical needs, we often overlook the body's need for touch. When we caress an infant, make love to our husband, or just snuggle the cat, we fulfill that important requirement. Studies have shown that senile elderly nursing home residents can be brought back to reality by being allowed to play with lovable puppies. Caring for pets has also been shown to be beneficial to criminals incarcerated for violent crimes. In nursing school I learned about one study showing that newborn infants who were deprived of physical nurturing failed to thrive and died! Keep that in mind, not only for your husband and children, but also for yourself. And take time to snuggle!

Who's in Control?

A final note about taking care of our bodies: If you don't control your body, it will surely control you. By looking at a person, you can tell who's in control! The Bible tells us that we can either be controlled by the flesh or by the Spirit—but not both.

> Do not be deceived, God is not mocked; for whatever a man sows, this he will also reap. For the one who sows to his own flesh shall from the flesh reap corruption, but the one who sows to the

Spirit shall from the Spirit reap eternal life—
Galatians 6:7,8.

I saw the truth of that scripture every day when I worked
as a registered nurse in the Intensive Care Unit of a hospital. I cared for people who were reaping what they had sown
for many years: the smokers with emphysema and lung can-
cer; the alcoholics with cirrhosis of the liver; and the obese
with every disease you could imagine. Their suffering
resulted from their bodies "reaping corruption."

Such loss of control over one's body doesn't happen over-
night; it happens day after day until it becomes a controlling
habit. A Spanish proverb says, "Habits are first cobwebs,
then cables." Fortunately, old negative habits can be
changed—one day at a time—until they become new positive habits.

If you have a negative habit that you want to change, you
can! You can do all things through Christ who strengthens
you! (See Philippians 4:13.) First, you must confess your sin
to God and ask Him to help you change. Then you must
make a moment-by-moment decision to live in the Spirit,
rather than in the flesh.

> Walk by the Spirit, and you will not carry out
> the desire of the flesh. For the flesh sets its desire
> against the Spirit, and the Spirit against the flesh;
> for these are in opposition to one another, so that
> you may not do the things that you please....
> Now those who belong to Christ Jesus have cru-
> cified the flesh with its passions and desires. If we
> live by the Spirit, let us also walk by the Spirit—
> Galatians 5:16,17,24,25.

When we offer our bodies to God as a "living sacrifice,"
He gives them back to us to enjoy—healthy and full of
energy! That helps us to be happier and more successful at
whatever we do. And that makes God happy, too.

Level Two: Mental/Emotional Needs

What would you be doing right now if you could do anything you wanted to? Would you be lazily swaying on a hammock in the back yard? Would you be lunching with friends? Or would you be creating some dazzling new outfit at your sewing machine? One of my favorite indulgences is to curl up in bed with a good book and a glass of juice. What are your favorite things to do? When did you last take the time to do one of them?

I hate to say it, but "All work and no play makes Mom a dull girl." Have you ever gotten so bogged down in cleaning the house and raising the kids that you feel like the mental equivalent of a two-year-old? Have you ever—like I once did—reached over and cut up your husband's meat on his plate, right in front of his parents? When you sink to that level, you begin to wonder if that brain in your head can still be salvaged. Rejoice, it can!

But it will take some effort on your part—effort to force yourself to make time for purely frivolous activities, just because you enjoy them. Take the time to do favorite nonproductive things, like listening to your vintage Johnny Mathis records while sorting through old photographs. See if you can spend an hour just counting the clouds from your patio recliner, or walking through the woods, or birdwatching. Do things that you used to enjoy as a child when you hadn't a worry in the world or a deadline to meet.

We all need to take time to enjoy the two things that every woman needs about as much as fish need water: beauty and a creative outlet. That's why so many women love to create things of beauty, either for their homes or for gifts. So take time to be creative in whatever genre you desire, whether it be gardening, decorating, making crafts, sewing, painting, writing, or whatever. One of the fringe benefits of being an at-home working woman is that you can incorporate creativity and beauty into every aspect of your daily work, whether it be cleaning the house, preparing meals, or clothing your family. So don't just do those things dutifully—approach them as exciting creative outlets!

And take the time to learn something new. Sign up for a gourmet cooking class, take a college course in anthropology, or learn how to hand dye and weave home-grown rabbit fur into gorgeous sweaters and shawls. (One local woman does that!) You could even take up skydiving if you want to! But do something to knock the cobwebs out of that overly-serious mind of yours. In the past few years I've learned many new skills by taking classes wherever they are available. In the process I learned about authentic Chinese cooking, gardening, making jewelry, public speaking, and quilting, to name a few. These activities have enriched my life, not only with new talents, but with new friends I met in the process.

It's also important to schedule a regular period during the week for what I call "Tune-Up Time." This is your special time to primp and preen. Perhaps every Thursday night you can arrange to have your husband put the children to bed while you take a long, relaxing, uninterrupted bath. Make it a luxurious event: dim the lights, burn a candle, and play soothing music as you bathe. See if you can stay in the water until your fingertips become all wrinkly. After your bath, slather on perfumed body lotion, condition and brush your hair, and give yourself a manicure and pedicure. You'll feel beautiful all week long. And your husband will enjoy the new you, too!

Above all, take the time to do things that make you laugh. Check out a video like *The Gods Must Be Crazy,* and watch it twice in a row. Play "Stinky Socks" with the kids. (That's where you take someone's dirty socks and chase each other around the house with them, yelling, "Stinky Socks!") Or best of all, get together with a friend who brings out the giggles in you. I have a couple of friends on whom I can always count to leave me breathless with laughter after only a short shopping trip. We may not impress others with our silliness, but we have entirely too much fun to care.

I've learned that postponing fun until tomorrow is a mistake because today is the only time you will ever enjoy it. My favorite season is autumn. I love the excitement of crisp, cool days and brilliant hillsides. Taking a long drive down the highway or a brisk walk in the park fills me with anticipation and exuberance. But I've often let an entire autumn season slip by without taking a single afternoon to enjoy it—just because I was too busy and thought I could do it tomorrow. Then it was winter! Those lovely autumn days can never be retrieved.

What's your favorite season? What's your favorite pastime? What would you most enjoy doing—even if you had just a few minutes to do it? Why don't you just go ahead and do it right now? And make it a regular part of your life.

Level Three: Spiritual Needs

If you practice every single helpful hint in this book and yet neglect what I've written in this section, you will have read this book in vain. Why? Because a relationship with God precedes every other need. With it people have been known to be happy with very little else. Without it, all the blessings in the world fail to satisfy.

A perfect example of the latter is someone whom I'll call Lisa. When I met Lisa she had everything money could buy. Her husband and children loved her very much. She had a magnificent home. She had no money problems. She was very attractive. She could do anything she wanted to do, whenever she wanted to do it. And yet Lisa was miserable.

She told me that she often suffered from acute depression. Even when she wasn't depressed, she was never satisfied. Nothing pleased her. When she came home from a vacation that most women would envy, I asked her if she had a good time. "No," she whined, "I couldn't find anything to buy."

Lisa was a classic example of someone who tried to fill that "God-shaped vacuum" in her with things. No matter how I tried to explain that she needed to fill the emptiness inside her with the Holy Spirit, she would not listen. Lisa was a spoiled, self-centered person who could only take. Therefore she would not give her life to Jesus. She knew that would mean taking Lisa off the throne of her life and putting Jesus there. She preferred her miserable emptiness to serving someone other than herself.

But most women who don't know Jesus as their Lord are not like Lisa. They aren't spoiled, nor are they self-centered. They are usually decent, lovable people who are doing the best they can to live a good life. They just don't know that living a good life is not enough to make them happy, nor to earn eternal salvation. They are not aware that Jesus said, "I am the way, and the truth, and the life; no one comes to the Father, but through Me" (John 14:6). They have never stopped to consider what that really means.

If you're one of those people, take a moment right now to think about who Jesus really is. Why is it that every time you write the date, you're writing how many years it has been since Jesus came to die on the cross for your sins? Is it just a coincidence? Or is it possible that God designed it as a divine reminder? Why does the world consider Jesus to be a good man if what He said about Himself was not true? Would a good man claim to be the only Son of God, the only one capable of forgiving your sins, and the only way to heaven if it were not true? If it is true, why haven't you received Him as your personal Lord and Savior? Have you ever taken the time to consider these things?

Is it possible that your feelings of failure, unhappiness, and insecurity are caused by knowing you have sinned against the God who created and loves you? No matter how hard you try, you can never be organized enough, successful enough, or perfect enough to erase those sins. But God has provided for your need. Only the blood of Jesus Christ can wash away those sins. When you ask Jesus to be your Savior, that blood He shed on the cross will immediately wash you as clean as snow. And God Himself never looks at them again!

That's why only those who are cleansed by the blood of Christ are fit to enter heaven when they die. Heaven is a perfect, sin-free place, and only those whose sins are washed away can enter there. God cannot dwell in the presence of sin. That is why God cannot dwell in you until you are free of sin. And the only way to be cleansed from your sin is to invite Jesus to come into your heart as your own personal Lord and Savior.

Wouldn't you like to invite Him in now? Wouldn't you like to experience real happiness? Wouldn't you like to enjoy a relationship with the Lord of Life? If so, simply pray the following prayer:

> Dearest Father in heaven, I lay my life before you now. I know I've failed you many times in the past. I've sinned against You and against others. Please forgive me for my sins. Wash them away with the blood of Jesus that was shed on the cross for me. Cleanse me now from all unrighteousness, and send the Holy Spirit to fill the emptiness in my heart.
>
> In return, Lord God, I promise to put Jesus on the throne of my heart. I will do all that I can to serve Him, rather than myself. I will read my Bible to learn what I can do to please You. I will join a church that teaches the Bible. And I will confess my sins to you in the future and receive your forgiveness day by day as I grow in the grace and knowledge of my Lord Jesus Christ.
>
> Jesus, I receive You into my heart now. I make You the Lord of my life. And I thank You for being my Savior, from this day forth. Amen.

If you just prayed that prayer, I rejoice for you! And so do the angels in heaven! Praise Jesus forevermore! A local Bible-believing church will be glad to encourage you in your new faith.

Although you may feel that this is the end of a long search, it's really just the beginning of an exciting, new life. Having Jesus Christ at the center of your being will add a new dimension to your role as a woman, wife, mother—and homemaker!

Suggested Reading

Kinnaman, Gary D. *And Signs Shall Follow.* Old Tappan, NJ: Chosen Books/Fleming H. Revell, 1987.

The best book I've read that addresses common controversies over the gifts of the Holy Spirit.

McDowell, Josh. *More Than a Carpenter.* Wheaton, IL: Tyndale House, 1977.

Good reading for those who want to know who Jesus really is.

Stoddard, Alexandra. *Living a Beautiful Life—500 Ways to Add Elegance, Order, Beauty and Joy to Every Day of Your Life.* New York: Avon Books, 1986.

How to make everyday activities into enjoyable events.

Swope, Dr. Mary Ruth. *Are You Sick and Tired of Feeling Sick and Tired?* Sprindale, PA: Whitaker House, 1984.

An excellent guide to health through better nutrition from a Christian perspective.

Notes

Chapter 1

1. *Focus on the Family* newsletter, April 1990, p. 1.
2. *Focus on the Family* magazine, October 1989, p. 5.
3. Larry Burkett, "How to Manage Your Money," Christian Financial Concepts, Issue 126, p. 6.
4. Sylvia Nasar, "Do We Live as Well as We Used To?" *Fortune,* September 14, 1987, p. 32-45.
5. Redbook, February 1989, p. 38.
6. Dennis Prager, "What Makes a Happy Person?" *Redbook,* February 1989, p. 77.

Chapter 3

1. Richard J. Foster, *The Celebration of Discipline* (New York: Harper & Row, 1978), p. 70.

Chapter 6

1. Edith Sitwell, *Fire of the Mind* (Michael Joseph, Ltd., London).

Chapter 11

1. David Wilkerson, *Set the Trumpet to Thy Mouth* (Lindale, TX: World Challenge, Inc., 1985), p. 67.
2. Gregg and Sono Harris, "The Rules of This House" Christian Life Workshops, 182 S.E. Kane Road, Gresham, OR. 97080.

Chapter 13

1. Bryant A. Stamford, Ph.D. and Porter Shimer, *Fitness Without Exercise* (New York: Warner Books, Inc. 1990).
2. Margaret Jensen, *First We Have Coffee* (San Bernadino, CA: Here's Life Publishers, 1982).
3. From an article written by Brian Banks in *Equinox*, reprinted in *Reader's Digest*, p. 176.
4. From an article written by Malcolm Gladwell, *Washington Post*, reprinted in *Reader's Digest*, p. 136.

About the Author

Linda Davis Zumbehl has worked as a registered nurse, real estate agent, and salesperson, but she always found homemaking to be her most enjoyable career. She loves to encourage homemakers in time management, organization, family values, and setting priorities through her "Homebodies" seminars. She also enjoys writing, quilting, and hot-air ballooning.

Her first book, *How to Be the Happy Wife of an Unsaved Husband,* shares scriptural insights and practical tips gleaned in waiting fifteen years for her husband's salvation. Linda has also appeared as a guest on *The 700 Club,* Trinity Broadcasting Network, and other television talk shows.

A lifetime resident of St. Louis, Linda has been married to her husband Mark for twenty-five years. They have two grown sons.

Would you like to share your favorite recipe, time-saving tip, or household hint with other homemakers? While I can't acknowledge every submission, I do appreciate your correspondence! Send your letters to:

Linda Davis Zumbehl
P. O. Box 973
Chesterfield, MO 63006